Spiritual Thoughts on Material Things

Thirty Days of Food for Thought

E. G. "Jay" Link

This book should be on the bookshelf of every Christian who desires to be a true follower of Jesus. It is not a book to be read, it is a book to be studied and pondered! Jay Link has written a masterpiece in an easy to read, warm style.

Ralph Palmen, President, Pinnacle Forum America

From his years of work with wealthy families, Jay Link uses Scripture and stories gathered from personal experience to provoke thinking about big life questions: accumulation of wealth, giving, generosity, stewardship, planning, and God-given purpose. His writing comes from a worldview shaped by studying the Holy Bible and allowing the Holy Spirit to inspire "spiritual thoughts on material things." As outlined in this book, Jay's counseling and teaching has inspired, challenged, and disciplined me to be a better servant in God's Kingdom—to work to multiply blessings and provision to other people from all that God has entrusted to me and my family.

**Bob Walker, Co-Owner & President,
Walker Manufacturing Co., Inc.**

Jay Link has devoted his life to helping the very affluent understand God's perspective on wealth and what He says about how to live a prosperous life. This book will be enormously valuable in challenging the thinking and broadening the horizons of everyone who is sincerely seeking to use all their resources in ways that will please God, increase their Kingdom impact, and promote healthy, family relationships.

**Howard Dayton, Co-Founder,
Crown Financial Ministries**

This book is scripturally based, filled with excellent stories, practical advice, and wise guidance. Jay has a very conversational and thought-provoking style of writing that caused me to ask the hard questions and wrestle with the answers. It is extremely comprehensive covering both the challenges and opportunities of being entrusted with much. I thought I might read it in 30 days. I'll probably be referencing it for 30 years.

Bill Williams, President, Generous Giving

This book combines Jay's gifts as a pastor, teacher, and planner with his passion for serving families and mobilizing resources to further God's Kingdom. All those who read this book will be challenged in their thinking, encouraged in their heart, and motivated to follow and apply God's principles of biblical stewardship. So, pull up a chair and for 30 days go on a journey with Jay as your guide, the Scriptures as your road map, and a biblical worldview as your context. You will be changed and His Kingdom furthered.

David Wills, President, National Christian Foundation

The Author

Mr. E. G. "Jay" Link has a unique blend of professional experience. He is both an ordained minister as well as a Family Wealth Counselor. Jay has spent decades helping wealthy families develop, implement, and then live out their strategic Master Stewardship Plans allowing them to maximize all that God has entrusted to them. It is his biblical knowledge and professional experience that uniquely qualifies him to authoritatively write, teach, and counsel on biblical stewardship for wealthy Christians.

Jay has personally trained and mentored hundreds of attorneys, accountants, money managers, and financial planners in Family Wealth Counseling for their clients, multiplying his ministry to wealthy families hundreds of times over. His first book, *Family Wealth Counseling: Getting to the Heart of the Matter*, and his Professional Mentoring Program training helped birth a nationwide revolution in wealth transfer planning that has radically changed the way many advisors now work with wealthy families.

Jay has an undying passion for showing wealthy Christian families how to effectively maximize their remaining time, employ their unique talents, and strategically deploy their accumulated treasures to expand and support the Kingdom of God. His family office firm, Kardia, Inc., works exclusively with affluent Christian families to help them develop, implement, and manage their customized, intergenerational Master Stewardship Plans. Its concierge family office approach, unique planning expertise, and Christian worldview make the firm extremely valuable as a long-term resource to the families it serves. With Kardia's hands-on guidance and attentive on-going support, its families are able to effectively and strategically steward all the resources that God has entrusted to them far beyond anything they ever imagined possible.

Spiritual Thoughts on Material Things
by E. G. "Jay" Link

Printed in the United States of America

ISBN 978-1-61579-015-9

Manuscript edited by Bethany Link, Dani Weaver, and Rick Killian.

Printed in the United States of America

16 15 14 13 12 11 10 09   1 2 3 4 5 6 7 8 9 10

www.xulonpress.com

Preface

There has been a philosophy dating back centuries that teaches that all things material are evil and all things spiritual are good. Hence, according to this thinking, if you really want to be spiritual, you will divest yourself of all your material possession, take a vow of poverty, and separate yourself as much as is humanly possible from the evil, material world. This thinking believes that money, not the *love* of money, is evil, and those who have successfully amassed a sizeable fortune are carnal, dishonest, and greedy.

Most pastors and ministers avoid teaching a proper perspective on material possessions because they themselves are not sure exactly what they believe about wealth. Having attended eight years of Bible college and seminary and having taken hundreds of hours of Bible and theology classes, I can say from personal experience that a biblical worldview on material things is not being taught at any of these levels of Christian education. Hence the silence on the subject in churches is almost deafening.

I have written this book to break the silence. I will speak plainly about your material things and challenge you to think spiritually about them. However, this book is not intended to only change the way you think, but even more importantly, to change the way you live—to give you a new perspective which will lead to a new way of handling the material things in your world.

I did not write this book to be read in one sitting. It is a thirty-day book. I would challenge you to give each daily reading the opportunity to soak into your mind and your heart. Allow time for the Holy Spirit to speak to you and for you to contemplate the thoughts for that day before you move on. At the end of each daily reading are three *Food for Thought* questions to help you consider the truths and applications of that day's reading. They are questions that may be hard to answer honestly. However, let me assure you that answering them honestly is a great way to begin to "take hold of that which is life indeed" (1 Timothy 6:17-19).

May this book provide you an abundance of new spiritual thoughts on your same old material things.

Table of Contents

Spiritual Thoughts on *Ownership*

Every animal in the forest belongs to me, and so do the cattle on a thousand hills. I know all the birds in the mountains, and every wild creature is in my care. If I were hungry, I wouldn't tell you, because I own the world and everything in it.

Psalm 50:10-12 CEV

Or do you not know that your body is a temple of the Holy Spirit who is in you, whom you have from God, and that you are not your own? For you have been bought with a price: therefore glorify God in your body.

1 Corinthians 6:19-20

Day 1

What Is My Relationship to My Stuff?

This is clearly the most foundational question we must answer if we are going to make any progress in our attitudes, perspectives, and decisions in relation to material things—particularly material wealth. If we cannot answer this question with clarity and confidence, we will find ourselves—in spite of our financial successes—underachieving in our lives. If you think of this question as a stool with three legs upon which the answer is balanced, you will be able to better envision the truth about your stuff.

Leg #1

The first "leg" of this stool is the fact that God owns everything because He created everything. King David tells us in Psalm 24:1, *"The earth is the Lord's and all it contains, the world, and those who dwell in it."* He goes on to add in Psalm 50:10-12 CEV,

Every animal in the forest belongs to me,
and so do the cattle on a thousand hills.
I know all the birds in the mountains,
and every wild creature is in my care.

If I were hungry, I wouldn't tell you,
because I own the world and everything in it.

Not only did God create everything that exists, He used all of His own materials to build it. So He truly is the only One who can claim to own anything.

If we build something, we may claim it is ours, but if we use someone else's materials to build it, then the owner of those materials can lay some claim to it as well. But in God's case, He not only dreamed it all up, He used His own creative materials to build it.

Leg #2

The second "leg" of this stool is the fact that not only did God create us, but He also redeemed us from slavery to the prince of this world through the death of His son, Jesus Christ. Paul tells us in Titus 2:13b-14, "*Christ Jesus, who gave Himself for us to redeem us from every lawless deed, and to purify for Himself a people for His own possession, zealous for good deeds.*"

This word *redeem* that Paul uses here is no longer commonly used in our culture today. When I was a young boy it was used often. I remember going to the grocery store with my mother. At the checkout counter, she would be given a certain number of S&H Green Stamps depending on how large her grocery purchase was. The reason I remember this so well is because I was charged with the task of licking those "tasty" little stamps and then putting them into the books.

My mother had a catalog filled with all kinds of products—everything from small kitchen appliances to a car. I was hoping my mother was not saving stamps for the car because it was several thousand Green Stamp books. I could see my tongue being forever stuck to the roof of my mouth from licking that many stamps! What made the Green

Stamp catalog so unusual was that instead of having prices for each item, it had the number of S&H Green Stamp books needed. A hand mixer might be four and a half books and a television 120 books. Do you remember the name of the place where you went to get these products? It was called the *Redemption Center*. It was the place where you would take your Green Stamp books to *redeem* the item you wanted. In other words, you traded in your stamp books for something you wanted to own.

This is what God did with Jesus. God was willing to redeem us by offering the blood of His own Son, so He could again own us—"*a people for His own possession.*" You see, God owns Christians twice—once because He made us and the second time because He bought us back after we were lost.

One last thought on this leg: what was the reason Paul gave in Titus 2:14 for why God was willing to redeem us? It was so we could be "*zealous for good deeds.*" Keep that thought in mind as we will be discussing this later in the book.

Leg #3

The final "leg" is the fact that we own nothing. We are called by God to be *stewards*, carrying out the Owner's wishes for *His* property. It is at this point that we need to come to grips with the terribly misused and abused concept of *stewardship*.

Before I focus on what stewardship does mean, let me tell you what it does not mean. Churches routinely use the term *stewardship* to refer to their capital campaigns. These campaigns are simply fundraisers used to get church members to give. But since "fundraiser" has such a negative connotation, they substitute (incorrectly) the seemingly nobler phrase "stewardship drive."

You will often hear churches and pastors use *steward-ship* as a synonym for *tithing*. I have seen in many church papers and bulletins the term *stewardship* used as a heading to report the weekly offerings and attendance. All of these uses that link *stewardship* to giving and tithing are inadequate at best—and entirely wrong at worst.

By definition, a *steward* is "a person who manages another's property or financial affairs; one who administers anything as the agent of another or others, a manager." So, for us to be "stewards for God," we must acknowledge that *all* we are and *all* we have possession of belongs to Him. We are charged with managing *His* property according to *His* wishes.

You can see that stewardship is not at all a synonym for tithing and fundraising; it is actually the opposite. *Tithing* has to do with what you *give*; *stewardship* has to do with what you *keep*. In other words, it is about how you manage everything that you have been entrusted to oversee. What most people miss is that stewardship is more about how you manage what is left over *after* you give than it is about *what you give*.

The radical, biblical concept of *stewardship* is easy enough to understand intellectually. However, it is anything but easy to consistently apply and live out. So what is your relationship to your stuff? *You are not the owner; you are merely the caretaker of somebody else's property.* And it is your job to manage *all* of it according to the Owner's wishes. Now, that really changes the game, does it not?

Some *Food for Thought* Questions

1. Until now, what has been your attitude about the ownership of your assets?
2. What are you going to do about being a manager instead of the owner?
3. How well are you managing what the Lord has entrusted to you according to His wishes?

Day 2

Keeping the Heart of God at the Heart of Living

Ican think of no better way to define what stewardship really is than with this phrase—*keeping the heart of God at the heart of living.* As we have seen, stewardship is all about carrying out the wishes of the Owner. The Owner is God and we are merely the caretakers of His property. As we saw yesterday, Psalm 24:1 states it clearly, *"The earth is the Lord's and all it contains, the world and all who live in it."* I think this encompasses everything we will ever get our hands on in this lifetime.

As I have said, this concept of stewardship is critically important, yet so often misunderstood. Even those who *intellectually* acknowledge that God owns everything do not *functionally* live as though He does. Let me illustrate my point by asking you to choose which one of the three questions below is the question we should be asking in regards to our material possessions.

1. What do I want to do with all my wealth?
2. What do I want to do with God's wealth?
3. What does God want me to do with His wealth?

No doubt you chose #3 as the proper question. In about thirty years of asking this question, every believer chooses #3. Intellectually, everyone is able to get this part of it. But practically speaking, we live as though #2 was the right question. We are more than happy to acknowledge that it all belongs to God, but when it comes to making decisions about what to do with what we oversee, we seldom, if ever, seek direction from the Owner.

Let me offer a few simple questions that should demonstrate just how true this is.

- When you bought your last car, did you ask God if this is the car He wanted you to buy with His money?
- When your money manager proposed an investment portfolio for you, did you go to the Lord and ask Him if these were the places He wanted His money invested?
- The last time you went shopping for clothes, did you ask your Father if these were the clothes He wanted you to wear?

Or, here is a question that will certainly apply to us all.

- Did we check with God to see if He wanted us to over-indulge His dwelling place with that last meal?

I hope you see my point. We are all routinely guilty of intellectually acknowledging that God owns everything, while we live, spend, and invest like it is all our own. The cornerstone of stewardship is full acknowledgment and consistent practice of allowing God to direct what He wants done with what He has entrusted us to manage.

I have recently been struck quite seriously with the reality that *all* our sin, at its core, is the result of personal selfishness. I would encourage you to ponder this yourself for a moment. As I have mulled this idea over and over in my mind, I have yet to find any exception. The truth is: we are our own worst enemies. We are continually getting in the way of God's best because we are so consumed with our desires, our rights, our dreams, our passions, and our way that we continually fall into sins of either commission (doing the wrong thing) or omission (not doing the right thing). Think about it. Why do we lie? Why do we cheat? Why do we steal? Why are we afraid? Why do we hate? Why do we commit adultery? Why do we lose our temper? Why do we become addicted to drugs, work, and entertainment? Why do we covet what others have? Why do we wear "masks" around others? Why do we not want to submit to God? I could go on and on, but it always circles back around to self. As the cartoon character Pogo confessed, "We have met the enemy and he is us."

The reason I am making this point is to say that our practical rejection of a life of devoted stewardship is just another example of how *self* gets in the way of God's best for us. We want to be in charge. We want to make the decisions. We want to "pull the trigger" and get things done. In ignoring the reality that we are nothing more than mere low-level managers who are expected to meticulously carry out the wishes of the all-loving and all-powerful Owner, our personal will, wishes, choices, and decisions prove to be categorically irrelevant to the discussion.

Someone once noted that at the center of SIN is the letter "I." We will always find "I"—self, ego, always looking out for number one—at the center of our sin.

- This is why Jesus said that if we really want to live, we must first die to self. *"For whoever wants to save his life will lose it, but whoever loses his life for me will find it"* (Matthew 16:25 NIV).
- If you want to be first, you must let everyone else go ahead of you. As the scripture says, *"The last will be first, and the first last"* (Matthew 20:16 ESV).
- If you want to be really free, you must submit to slavery. *"Whoever wants to become great among you must be your servant, and whoever wants to*

be first must be your slave" (Matthew 20:26-27 NIV).

- If you want to be great, you must strive to make everyone else greater than yourself. *"Do nothing out of selfish ambition or vain conceit, but in humility consider others better than yourselves"* (Philippians 2:3 NIV, see also Luke 9:48).

It is all about death to self.

The reason stewardship is so challenging to practice is that we must get *self* out of the way. As long as we are fallen creatures with a fallen nature, we will have to wrestle daily with the lingering ghosts of our own selfishness until we someday finally shed this "dirt body" and move on to better things. In the mean time, we must resist with every ounce of our being the temptation to inappropriately assume the throne and play little gods over stuff that does not even belong to us.

Some *Food for Thought* Questions

1. What areas of your life are most difficult for you to relinquish control?
2. How have you seen selfishness in your own life sabotage God's best for you?
3. What is it about God's ownership of your stuff that seems most restricting to you?

Day 3

What About Everything Else?

We have spent the first two days contemplating our relationship to our material wealth, but that is really only a small portion of all we steward. The Bible gives us several other possessions that we do not own, but are called to carefully manage. In order for us to hear, "Well done," as we relocate to Heaven, we will need to diligently manage these other assets as well.

Caretakers of a Brief Allotment of Time

Someone once said, "I can tell you a lot about people's priorities in life by simply looking at two things—their checkbook and their calendar." Even though in our current high tech culture, we likely no longer write too many checks or have a day-timer, the principal is still the same. How you choose to spend your time and your money reveals what is really important to you. It is important to keep in mind that you do "spend" your time in the same way you spend money. You will exchange your time for something and the time that has been spent is gone once and forever.

Paul commands us in Ephesians 5:15-17, *"Therefore be careful how you walk, not as unwise men but as wise, making the most of your time, because the days are evil. So then do not be foolish, but understand what the will of the Lord is."* Here we go again, using our time according to the will of the

Lord. Why? Because it is His time on loan to us. He wants us to not just spend it, but to invest it wisely for eternity.

Most people do not know that Moses actually wrote one of the Psalms. If you notice the title to Psalm 90, you will see it is written by Moses. He prays to God, *"So teach us to number our days, that we may present to You a heart of wisdom"* (v. 12).

I met a man many years ago that tried to take this prayer seriously. He determined his actuarial life expectancy and then created a calendar with the remaining number of days he had left to live. It may seem silly, but being reminded each day that today you have one less day than you did yesterday is extremely appropriate in helping us number our days.

There was a professor at the Christian college where I taught who would always answer when you asked how he was, "I'm better than yesterday because I am one day closer to Heaven!" He had learned to number his days.

Caretakers of a Slowly Decaying Body

Unless you are still in your twenties, your body is on the decline and you probably are quite aware of it. Mortality, death, and decay were a major part of the curse on humanity because of the fall of Adam. This has left us with the stewardship responsibility for the care and feeding of these "earthly tents" in which we are temporarily trapped.

Paul asked a rhetorical question in 1 Corinthians 6:19-20, *"Do you not know that your body is a temple of the Holy Spirit who is in you, whom you have from God, and that you are not your own? For you have been bought with a price: therefore glorify God in your body."* Here we are faced with the reality that we have been redeemed (bought back) and God now owns our bodies twice over.

Even though these bodies are ultimately destined to break down and cease to function, we are still called by God to do everything we can to care for and maintain these temporary "dwellings" to the best of our abilities. How we eat and how we exercise, for example, should not be a matter of personal preferences, but a matter of God's directives. Abusing, neglecting, or ignoring our bodies is an act of poor stewardship which does not please the true Owner. Let me ask you, if you loaned something to someone and they brought it back to you damaged, would you be happy with the person to whom you had loaned it? I think not.

I have learned one very important reality in my own efforts to properly care for and feed God's body: your spiritual well-being is *definitely* tied to your physical well-being. I am not sure how that works, but I have seen it time and time again in my own life. When I am doing well physically, I am also doing well spiritually.

Paul challenges us in Romans 12:1, *"Therefore I urge you, brethren, by the mercies of God, to present your bodies a living and holy sacrifice, acceptable to God, which is your spiritual service of worship."* Is how you treat your body an act of worship? Is it a demonstration of your careful management of God's property?

Caretakers of the Good News of Salvation

God has done a number of things that from a purely human perspective seem to be less than optimal in His plans for us and eternity. For example, one thing that troubles me about God's plan is why He put us in charge of getting His message out. I mean, He is God. He had unlimited means at His disposal to let the world know about the way of salvation. Yet somehow in His divine wisdom, He chooses to use *us*, imperfect as we are, to spread the Good News of salvation. It strikes me as being very inefficient if He really wanted to get as many people as possible to Heaven.

27

Nonetheless, that is His plan for the Good News of Christ. It is obvious Paul understood this as he shares in 1 Corinthians 4:1-2, "*Let a man regard us in this manner, as servants of Christ and stewards of the mysteries of God. In this case, moreover, it is required of stewards that one be found trustworthy.*" He goes on to say in 9:16-17, "*For if I preach the gospel, I have nothing to boast of, for I am under compulsion; for woe is me if I do not preach the gospel. For if I do this voluntarily, I have a reward; but if against my will, I have a stewardship entrusted to me.*"

There we see it again. We have been entrusted to spread someone else's message—like it or not. We are caretakers of the Gospel and we need to spread it anywhere we can to anyone who will listen. That is quite a demanding commission, but it is at the core of our purpose on the earth.

There is one final aspect of this Gospel management responsibility that I want to mention in closing. Peter reminds us that as managers of God's grace, we are to use the gifts and talents that God has loaned us for His purposes. Look at 1 Peter 4:10, "*As each one has received a special gift, employ it in serving one another as good stewards of the manifold grace of God.*" We are charged with spreading the Word and serving fellow believers with the abilities we are entrusted with.

As you can see, stewardship covers every single aspect of our lives on this earth. How well are you stewarding all that God has entrusted to your care and management?

Some *Food for Thought* Questions

1. How often do you consult with God about how you are currently spending your time?
2. Is the current condition of your physical body a reflection of your careful management of this precious resource that has been temporarily loaned to you?

3. How well are you managing your opportunities to share the good news of Christ with others?

Spiritual Thoughts on *Prosperity*

"For I know the plans I have for you," declares the LORD," *plans to prosper you and not to harm you, plans to give you hope and a future."*

Jeremiah 29:11 NIV

From everyone who has been given much, much will be required; and to whom they entrusted much, of him they will ask all the more.

Luke 12:48b

Day 4

Why Do Some People Prosper Materially While Others Do Not? (Part 1)

The Apostle John reports in John 12:1-8 an emotionally touching story as Jesus enters the final week before His crucifixion:

> Six days before the Passover, Jesus arrived at Bethany, where Lazarus lived, whom Jesus had raised from the dead. Here a dinner was given in Jesus' honor. Martha served, while Lazarus was among those reclining at the table with him. Then Mary took about a pint of pure nard, an expensive perfume; she poured it on Jesus' feet and wiped his feet with her hair. And the house was filled with the fragrance of the perfume. But one of his disciples, Judas Iscariot, who was later to betray him, objected, "Why wasn't this perfume sold and the money given to the poor? It was worth a year's wages." He did not say this because he cared about the poor but because he was a thief; as keeper of the money bag, he used to help himself to what was put into it. "Leave her alone," Jesus replied. "It was intended that she should save this perfume for the day of my burial. You will always have the poor among you, but you will not always have me."

This story has a number of very valuable lessons for us. In fact, this passage itself could be a series of great sermons. However, there is one phrase in this story that is seldom considered that I want us to consider. It is Jesus' statement, *"You will always have the poor among you."* Jesus made this statement about 2,000 years ago and in reality it is still just as true today as it was back then. We still have the poor among us. The only difference is that there are now more poor living on this planet than there were in Jesus' day.

Since poor people have walked this earth almost from the beginning of the human race and they still are among us to this day, here are some challenging questions for us to consider:

- Why are we not one of them?
- Why is it that some people prosper materially while others do not?
- Why are we rich when most of the world, by and large, is so poor?

I think these are important questions worth our asking and I think it is even more important that we attempt to answer them from a biblical perspective.

They Must Be Given the *Opportunity* to Prosper

Let me pose what I believe to be another very profound question: "Of all the times and all the places in the world that you and I could have been born, why were we born at this specific time and place in all of human history?" In other words, "Why here? Why now? Why us?"

I have had the privilege to travel to many places in the world and I have personally witnessed levels of abject poverty that are difficult to even observe, much less describe. I have been to places where common workers make $1 a day while skilled workers make $2.50 a day when they can find the work. There are no pictures or words that adequately capture the depths of poverty these people somehow survive.

Many of these people are very bright, intelligent, and incredibly resourceful—they have to be even to stay alive. Yet, their opportunity to succeed in accumulating any material prosperity is zero. Either the form of their government or their culture prevents it from happening.

Let me give you one example from Tanzania, Africa. The culture in Tanzania is very strong on family responsibility. Because of this, if an individual creates a successful business or begins to get ahead financially, relatives he or she has never even met will come out of the woodwork and expect to be supported. These relatives are not looking for a job so much as a handout. It is an attitude that goes so far as to believe that if you have two pairs of socks (or any other thing, for that matter) and I have none, then it is your duty to give me one of them. If someone figures out how to get ahead financially, then culturally-speaking, all of their extended family will feel they have the right to seek financial assistance and expect the prospering individual to help them all. It is a cultural burden that kills any incentive to get ahead, hindering everyone from doing more than what it takes to merely survive. While I saw this myself in Tanzania, friends have told me it is true of other places in Africa as well.

This is their culture's social welfare program—an extreme form of communism that is a societal and cultural curse. Needless to say for every financially successful Tanzanian, he or she has hundreds of extended family members who are financially destitute. So, from the time they are small children, the ambitious are trained to think, "Why should I work hard and try to accumulate anything if all I end up doing is giving it away to family members who will never contribute anything to earning it? I might as well spend it as soon as I earn it or not work so hard in the first place." You see, these cultural mores prevent any motivation for a person to get ahead financially even when given the opportunity.

The story of Esther is instructive for us here. Esther, a Jewish girl, providentially becomes Queen of Persia. Haman, a high government official, has launched a plot to exterminate all the Jews in the lands where Persia rules. Mordecai, Esther's uncle, learns of the plot and meets with Esther to ask her to intervene to stop the genocide (which would include herself). He puts this crisis and Esther's providential ascension to Queen of Persia into a larger perspective. In Esther 4:14b, he says to her, "*And who knows whether you have not attained royalty for such a time as this?*"

I have heard it said many times over the years from people we have worked with, "I feel like my whole life has just been preparation for what God wants me to do right now."

Could it be that in God's wisdom and providence He has provided you an opportunity to attain prosperity for just "*such a time as this?*"

Could it be the reason God has chosen to place you in this country at this time in human history is because He has a divine purpose for giving you this rare opportunity to succeed financially and to prosper? Paul tells us in Acts 17:26 NIV, "*From one man He made every nation of men, that they should inhabit the whole earth; and He determined the times set for them and the exact places where they should live.*" You see, God has a plan and you are part of the blessing He seeks to extend to others.

We are here now, not by our choice or by our own will, but because an almighty, all-wise God, "*created* [our] *inmost being and knit* [us] *together in our mothers' womb*" (Psalm 139:13 NIV) so He could bring us into this world for such a time as this.

Why have you been blessed with such an incredible opportunity? I will tell you why. *It is just a gift.*

Some *Food for Thought* Questions

1. Why has God placed you in America at this time in history?
2. Why has God blessed you by giving you the opportunity to amass such an abundance of surplus wealth?
3. What does He want you to do with this gift of opportunity?

Day 5

Why Do Some People Prosper Materially While Others Do Not? (Part 2)

They Must be Given the *Abilities* to Prosper.

When I use the term *abilities*, I could just as easily use the word *gifts*. I remember what I heard a coach say once, "Hard work and dedication are critical to success, but neither is a substitute for talent." My personal sports career confirms that hard work and dedication without a substantial dose of talent will make you at best an average athlete. There is just no substitute for natural, God-given *ability*. We all know people with tons of natural talent in some area in which they excel with little effort.

I have identified five unique abilities that are common among those who achieve financial prosperity.

1. They have been given the needed *intelligence*.

Now I know intelligence is a relative term. And I, for one, have never paid excessive attention to IQ tests, because the grade one gets is not always a good indicator of that person's actual intelligence (i.e., Einstein).

A man once shared this comment with me. He said, "The A students become the teachers, and the B students go to work for the C students." In other words, success in school and on tests is not what intelligence is all about. If you think about it, there is a lot of truth to that. You do not have to be the "brightest bulb on the tree" to succeed, but you do at least need to be above average.

Have you ever asked yourself, why did God choose to give me such a good mind while not giving it to others? I will tell you why. It is just a *gift*.

2. They have been given the needed *work ethic*.

A number of years ago, I attended a convention of about 1,000 very successful business owners. A psychologist/executive coach was speaking and he asked this interesting question, "How many of you had your first real, paying job by the time you were eleven years old?" I was absolutely amazed; almost every single hand in the room went up. His point was that a motivation to work has been embedded in the personality of every financially successful person. That motivation produces the work ethic that continues to develop throughout their lives.

Before I was eleven, I was mowing lawns, delivering newspapers, and selling greeting cards door to door with my little red wagon behind me full of samples. God just gives some both the drive and the passion to work. It is something most wealthy people have been doing for many years now. You see, it is just a *gift*.

3. They have been given the needed *vision*.

You will remember Robert F. Kennedy expressed it this way, "There are those who look at things the way they are, and ask 'Why?' I dream of things that never were, and ask 'Why not?'"

Being able to see something in the future that does not yet exist is a gift only a very few are given. I am always amazed when I visit a manufacturing plant. I observe what they build and think, "How in the world did they ever think up how to create this product? How did they figure out how to build it?"

Once I asked an owner of a manufacturing plant about how they came up with the way to build their product. He said, "Oh, it's not all that difficult." Nonsense! It *is* all that difficult. This man has the special ability to see what is not and bring what he sees into existence. How can people do that? I will tell you how. It is just a *gift*.

4. They have been given the needed *courage*.

As often as President Obama repeated during his campaign that he wants to redistribute the wealth in America (taking it from the *Haves* and giving it to the *Have Nots*), he admitted in his inaugural address that it will be the "risk takers" that will get us out of the mess that our country is currently in.

Psychologists tell us that risk taking is not just a learned behavior; it is the way certain people are wired. It is part of who they are. The thrill of the risk of winning big or losing big is exhilarating for risk takers. They thrive on the adventure, the danger, and on "hitting the grand slam."

Relatively speaking, there are not many people like that in this world—ones who have this special wiring and who are not afraid to take a chance. Do you know why? Because it is just a *gift*.

5. They have been given the needed *common sense*.

I am not sure how many of you have ever heard of the Darwin Awards. It is a website that bestows its annual awards to people who have done exceedingly dumb things (proving, they say, that we must have evolved from apes through a process of the survival of the fittest and the demise of the dumbest). Most of the winners receive the recognition posthumously because they died from their award-winning mishap. If you have never visited their website, you might find it quite entertaining.

You have likely met many people during your lifetime who as my dad used to say, "...did not have enough sense to come in out of the rain." We would all agree that not everyone is endowed with an adequate amount of common sense, especially when it comes to being materially prosperous in life.

Even though I imagine each of us have some entertaining stories we could tell about some of the dumb things we have done during our lifetimes confirming that we did not graduate first in the common sense class either, we did at least graduate. Why do you have such good common sense? I will tell you why. It is just a *gift*.

If God does not give them the needed *intelligence*, the required *work ethic*, the ability to be *visionaries*, wire them to be *risk-takers*, and give them a high level of *common sense*, then even if the person has the opportunity to prosper, He will not. Our country is full of people who have had every opportunity to succeed, but they struggle and fail because even though they have the opportunity, they do not have the abilities. That is because these abilities are gifts from God.

Some *Food for Thought* Questions

1. How can possessing this special combination of abilities cause you to "think more highly of yourself than you ought" (see Romans 12:3)?

2. How should the reality that you possess all these abilities actually keep you humble?

3. Since God has chosen to hard-wire you with such a unique combination of abilities, how might you be using

them to have an even greater Kingdom impact than you are now?

Day 6

Why Do Some People Prosper Materially While Others Do Not? (Part 3)

They Must Be Given the *Power* to Prosper.

This unique gift from God is the least understood and possibly the most important for us to grasp. The Bible tells us that there are actually three powers God gives us regarding wealth accumulation. Unless He gives us all three, our lives will be unhappy, out of balance, and self-absorbed—no matter how prosperous we are.

Power #1: The Power to *Make Wealth*.

Deuteronomy 8:18 is a verse that every financially successful Christian ought to have hanging somewhere on one of his walls. In this verse God says, *"But you shall remember the LORD your God, for it is* He *who is giving you power to make wealth."*

Paul says it this way in 2 Thessalonians 1:11-12 NIV, *"That our God may count you worthy of His calling, and that by His power He may fulfill every good purpose of yours and every act prompted by your faith."* God gives some the power to accumulate great amounts of wealth while fulfilling those good purposes.

If God gives you the power to make wealth, you will make it. It is that simple. For people who have this power, they are like Midas — whatever they set their hand to do turns into gold. If God does not give someone this power, no matter how hard that person might try, no matter what opportunities he may be presented, and no matter what abilities he has, he will not become rich.

Solomon clearly understood this. He tells us in Proverbs 23:4-5, "*Do not weary yourself to gain wealth, cease from your consideration of it. When you set your eyes on it, it is gone. For wealth certainly makes itself wings like an eagle that flies toward the heavens.*" For the person without this power, wealth will never become anything more than the illusive "pot of gold" at the end of the proverbial rainbow.

Wealthy families face a myriad of challenges, dangers to the family, ever-present stress, and grave responsibility that accompanies possessing wealth. As each of you knows all too well, having wealth is not all that it is imagined to be by those who do not have it. It is a huge responsibility entrusted to only a few. Jesus points this out in Luke 12:48 TLB, "*Much is required from those to whom much is given, and much more is required from those to whom much more is given.*" As *The Message* puts it, "*Great gifts mean great responsibilities; greater gifts, greater responsibilities!*"

Whenever I have talked with the builders of wealth, whether they are followers of Jesus or not, there is one common acknowledgment in almost every case among them. The follower of Jesus will use the term "blessed" to describe their success, while a non-Christian will use the words "lucky" or "fortunate." Almost everyone who has achieved a significant level of wealth recognizes that the success they have achieved is really disproportionate to the personal genius and hard work that they have put into it.

And in all this, we must never forget Deuteronomy 8:17 which cautions, "*You may say in your heart, 'My power and the strength of my hand made me this wealth.'"* This simply is not true. This is the ultimate in self-pride and God warns us in Proverbs 16:18 NIV, *"Pride goes before destruction, a haughty spirit before a fall."* How is it that you have the power to make wealth? God tells us. It is just a *gift.*

Power #2: The Power to *Enjoy Wealth.*

This power is not commonly discussed, but Solomon makes a startling observation for us in Ecclesiastes 5:19, *"Furthermore, as for every man to whom God has given riches and wealth, He has also empowered him to eat from them and to receive his reward and rejoice in his labor; this is the gift of God."* God also gives us the power to enjoy the wealth we have accumulated.

Solomon adds that not all those who have the power to make wealth have the power to enjoy it. In Ecclesiastes 6:1-2 Solomon observes, *"There is an evil which I have seen under the sun and it is prevalent among men—a man to whom God has given riches and wealth and honor so that his soul lacks nothing of all that he desires; yet God has not empowered him to eat from them."* He has the wealth, but he cannot enjoy it.

Solomon is telling us that there are people that, no matter how rich they become, they still think and act like they are poor. I remember many years ago, an elderly gentleman needed a surgical procedure for his eyes which cost $5,000. He would not have the surgery done, even though he had over $1 million in his retirement plan. He just could not spend any of his accumulated wealth even for his own health. His wealth was no use to him. He might as well have been poor. He had the power to make wealth, but God had not given him the power to benefit from it.

Solomon gives us another sad example of someone who has the power to make wealth but not to enjoy it in Ecclesiastes 4:8. Here he observes,

> *There was a certain man without a dependent, having neither a son nor a brother, yet there was no end to all his labor. Indeed, his eyes were not satisfied with riches and he never asked, "And for whom am I laboring and depriving myself of pleasure?" This too is vanity and it is a grievous task.*

You see the power to make wealth without the power to enjoy it neutralizes the blessing of wealth and instead turns it into a curse. This becomes the perfect contrast between the person who possesses wealth and the person whose wealth possesses him.

In Ecclesiastes 2:24-26 Solomon tells the fate of those with the power to make wealth, but not to enjoy it,

> *There is nothing better for a man than to eat and drink and tell himself that his labor is good. This also I have seen that it is from the hand of God. For who can eat and who can have enjoyment without Him? For to a person who is good in His sight He has given wisdom and knowledge and joy, while to the sinner He has given the task of gathering and collecting so that he may give to one who is good in God's sight. This too is vanity and striving after wind.*

Solomon adds further in Ecclesiastes 5:18, "*Here is what I have seen to be good and fitting: to eat, to drink and enjoy oneself in all one's labor in which he toils under the sun during the few years of his life which God has given him; for this is his reward.*"

By contrast, Solomon sees some who go so far as to even try to hide their accumulated wealth in Proverbs 13:7 NIV, *"One man pretends to be rich, yet has nothing; another pretends to be poor, yet has great wealth."*

Many affluent people have long refused to enjoy the wealth God has empowered them to accumulate because they falsely believe that there is something wrong with being wealthy or they are plagued with a nagging fear that something might happen and they could someday lose it all. You need to happily embrace the prosperity you have. However, you need be careful that you do not enjoy more of it that the Master intended. Because, you see, there is still one more power.

Power #3: The Power to *Give Wealth.*

Both the Old Testament and the New Testament give us a telling illustration of what happens when all three of these powers are not bestowed upon and embraced by a wealth builder.

Solomon observes in Ecclesiastes 5:13 NIV, *"I have seen a grievous evil under the sun: wealth hoarded to the harm of its owner."* He made it and he enjoyed it, but he has either not been given or refused to accept the third power—to give it. And when this happens the person's accumulated wealth becomes his enemy.

Jesus uses a painful illustration with the wealthy farmer in Luke 12:18-19. The farmer after a bumper crop says, *"Here's what I'll do: I'll tear down my barns and build bigger ones. Then I'll gather in all my grain and goods, and I'll say to myself, Self, you've done well! You've got it made and can now retire. Take it easy and have the time of your life!"* (THE MESSAGE). He had the power to make wealth and certainly to enjoy it—but the thought never crossed his mind to give

47

away any of his vast surplus. And that is why Jesus called this man a "fool."

Romans 12:6-8a NIV reminds us,

> *We have different gifts, according to the grace given us. If a man's gift is prophesying, let him use it in proportion to his faith. If it is serving, let him serve; if it is teaching, let him teach; if it is encouraging, let him encourage; if it is contributing to the needs of others, let him give generously.*

2 Corinthians 9:11 should be a clarion call to unreserved generosity, "*He will make you rich in every way so that you can always give freely*" (NCV).

I really appreciate what Anne Frank, the Jewish girl who lived during the holocaust observed, "No one has ever become poor by giving." I have pondered her comment often and I have not come up with any exception to her statement. I think if we are honest, all of us have occasionally experienced some degree of fear or anxiety that if we really got wildly generous with our accumulated wealth we could someday end up with not enough for ourselves.

Paul reveals God's purpose for making people wealthy in 1 Timothy 6:17-19. He commands Timothy to,

> *Instruct those who are rich in this present world not to be conceited or to fix their hope on the uncertainty of riches, but on God, who richly supplies us with all things to enjoy. Command them to do good, to be rich in good works, to be generous and ready to share, storing up for themselves the treasure of a good foundation for the future, so that they may take hold of that which is life indeed.*

You see it is in the giving that we find *"life indeed."* It is not in the making and it is not in the enjoying, but *"life indeed"* is realized in the *giving.*

Remember, Paul tells Titus in 2:13-14, *"Christ Jesus, who gave Himself for us to redeem us from every lawless deed, and to purify for Himself a people for His own possession, zealous for good deeds."* We have been redeemed to be busy doing good deeds and God has blessed only a very few among men to enjoy the opportunity to be busy not just doing good deeds, but doing great deeds—deeds that are worthy of the gifts that God has bestowed upon them.

To enjoy the power of giving we must understand that our fundamental objective and primary purpose for accumulating possessions is *to give them away.* As we all need to occasionally be reminded, sooner or later we will be giving them all away anyway—why not do it with joy?

You can remember these three financial powers with the medical term—EKG: *Earning* wealth, *Keeping* wealth, and *Giving* wealth. To be healthy, affluent Christians, we need to have a healthy EKG.

For those who have already become prosperous, God has obviously given them the *opportunity* to make wealth, the *abilities* to make wealth, and the *power* to make wealth. So you may ask, "Why do I need to know this now? I am already wealthy. Thanks for the Bible lesson."

There are two applications that I hope to make from all of this. The first application is that your accumulated wealth is a *gift.* By God's wisdom you were placed in America in her richest days. By His grace you were given the needed natural gifts to succeed. By His omnipotent power you were empowered to make wealth. What He has materially done for you ought to humble you before Him. If you think about it, you are at best only a willing and faithful participant in God's plan to prosper you. You must never forget that you are not the *cause* of your prosperity—you are merely the *beneficiary* of it.

And that leads me to my second application. Let me introduce this application with a question. It is not a question that you may be able to immediately answer, but it is a question that we all need to ask and it is even more importantly a question we all need to be able to answer. *Does your vision for the Kingdom of God match your current financial capacity to fulfill that vision?*

Some people I have met over the years have been given such an extraordinary vision for the Kingdom that it vastly exceeded their current, personal, financial capacity to fulfill it. You may know some people like that. Many of these visionaries end up beginning ministries or quitting their day jobs and leaving for a mission field. These people often have very limited financial resources. But what they do have is a surrendered life and an extraordinary vision.

Then there are other people who have a vision for the Kingdom of God that is substantially smaller than their current financial capacity to fulfill it. In other words they have more money than they have vision.

Now, let me ask the question in a different way: *Over the years, has your vision for the Kingdom of God continued to expand with your ever-increasing financial capacity?*

Let me give you a good, but admittedly extreme, example of this. Some years ago, I met a couple who had a very substantial net worth. I learned that they had recently been asked to consider contributing $20,000 to help print some Bibles for the ministry that had introduced us to them. I learned that it took them over three months of wrestling with the decision before they finally "pulled the trigger" and gave the money to print the Bibles.

You may think, "How bizarre." But here is what was really happening. This couple still thought about their Kingdom impact like they did twenty-five years earlier when they were only worth a miniscule fraction of what they are today—back when $20,000 would have been a lot of money. You see their vision for the Kingdom of God had not grown proportionately with their ever-increasing financial capacity. They had vastly more wealth than they had Kingdom vision.

It could be said this way, *a person whose financial capacity does not match or exceed his vision for the Kingdom is frankly living beneath his calling and his privilege.*

Is your vision for the Kingdom of God equal to or greater than your ability to fund that vision? In other words, *is your current vision for the Kingdom too small?*

Remember the verse I quoted earlier. Paul prays and this is my earnest prayer for each of you, "*May our God count you worthy of His calling, and that by His power He may fulfill every good purpose of yours and every act prompted by your faith.*" Just how big is your vision for the Kingdom?

Some *Food for Thought* Questions

1. Which of these three gifts (Earning, Keeping, or Giving) have you personally had the most trouble with? Why?
2. How often have you been tempted to credit your own efforts and talent for your financial successes?
3. How much does your vision for the Kingdom compare to your ability to financially fund that vision?

Day 7

Warning to the Wealthy: Coming to Christ Through the "Eye of a Needle"

We all know the story of the rich, young ruler (Matthew 19:16-30, Mark 10:17-31, Luke 18:18-30) who came to Jesus looking for eternal life only to find that the price to receive it was more than he was willing to pay. He went away sad and unsaved.

What is particularly instructive about this story is the follow up conversation Jesus has with his disciples. Matthew 19:23-24 reports, *"Then Jesus said to his disciples, 'I tell you the truth, it is hard for a rich man to enter the kingdom of heaven. Again I tell you, it is easier for a camel to go through the eye of a needle than for a rich man to enter the kingdom of God'"* (NIV).

This statement by Jesus is so troubling that many have tried to lessen its absolute exclusion by suggesting that when Jesus used the term "eye of a needle," He was referring to a small, narrow gate by the entrance of the main city gate that would be difficult (but not impossible) for a camel to get through. The problem is that neither historians nor archeologists have found any evidence whatsoever that this kind of narrow gate was ever referred to as an "eye of a needle."

Others who do not like the ramifications of Jesus' statement have suggested that the correct word is not "camel," but "rope"—suggesting that a rope could go through the eye of a needle if it was untangled allowing one strand at a time to be put through. This effort to substitute the word "rope" for "camel" is driven more by a dislike of the obvious meaning of Jesus' statement than an honest effort at a legitimate translation.

His disciples, several of whom were themselves well off, certainly understood His statement of the impossible because they were astonished by it and asked, "*'Who then can be saved?' Jesus looked at them and said, 'With man this is impossible, but with God all things are possible.'*" Peter pleaded, "*We have left everything to follow you!*" (Matthew 19:25-27a NIV). The disciples understood exactly what Jesus meant. They too were concerned about getting through the "eye."

The wealthy Christians I know are all committed followers of Jesus. So, you may ask, "Did these people somehow make it through the impossible 'eye of a needle'? Are they the exceptions?"

It is important that we distinguish between those who knew Christ before they became rich and those who have become rich having never known Christ. The wealthy families I am associated with became believers prior to being possessors of great wealth. Therefore they did not have all the "baggage" of wealth to prevent them from responding to the invitation of Christ. Their riches were gained more as a result of living a faithful and obedient life—being blessed by the Lord and trusted with material prosperity as one of His children.

Jesus in this passage is referring to people who have become rich without any personal relationship with God. He says for these "rich" people it is as impossible for them to enter into the Kingdom of God as it is for a camel to go through the eye of a needle.

Why? Why is it impossible? It is impossible because what riches characteristically does to a man makes it impossible for him to come to Christ. Jesus expresses this truth to us with His very first beatitude, *"Blessed are the poor in spirit, for theirs is the Kingdom of Heaven"* (Matthew 5:3 NIV). Simply stated, a "rich" man cannot come to Christ. Only a "poor man" can come to Christ. Here is why. Material riches prevent a man from recognizing his absolute spiritual poverty and his desperate need for a Savior.

This word "poor" that Jesus uses in this beatitude comes from the Greek word that means "to shrink, cower, or cringe," as beggars often did in Jesus' day. Classical Greek used the word to refer to a person who was reduced to total destitution, who was crouched in the corner begging, one hand reaching out while the other hand covers their face in shame. This term is not used to simply mean poor, but "begging" poor. It is the word used in Luke 16:20 to describe Lazarus.

The word normally used for poverty is a different word entirely and is used to describe the widow Jesus saw giving her offering at the Temple. She had very little, but she still had two small copper coins to give. (See Luke 21:2.)

Poverty of spirit comes when we recognize our total spiritual destitution and our complete dependence on God for everything. There is no saving resource in us. There is nothing that we can offer of value. We are left *begging poor* and our only recourse is to reach out our sin-sick hands and beg God for mercy and grace.

The story of the Pharisee and the tax collector in Luke 18:10-14 is the classic contrast between one who was rich in spirit and one who was poor in spirit. Jesus said,

Two men went up to the temple to pray, one a Pharisee and the other a tax collector. The Pharisee stood up and prayed about himself: "God, I thank you that I am not like other men—robbers, evildoers, adulterers—or even like this tax collector. I fast twice a week and give a tenth of all I get."

But the tax collector stood at a distance. He would not even look up to heaven, but beat his breast and said, "God, have mercy on me, a sinner."

I tell you that this man, rather than the other, went home justified before God. For everyone who exalts himself will be humbled, and he who humbles himself will be exalted.

None of us likes the idea of being poor in spirit. It is contrary to our fleshly, human nature. We do not want to think of ourselves that way.

So, poverty of spirit is a personal awareness and recognition before God that there is nothing in us, about us, or possessed by us that warrants any sense of self-sufficiency or provides any spiritual "credit" to our account. We are *begging poor* spiritually.

This being the case, exactly what is it about material riches that makes it in human terms impossible for its possessors to enter the Kingdom of God? There seems to be three damning illusions of riches that block their way.

The Damning Illusion of *Personal Security*

Wealthy people develop a conscious and unconscious sense of security in their accumulated wealth. They feel safe and secure behind their mountains of assets. They know that they have so much excess that no matter what happens they will be fine.

Solomon, a very rich man himself, observes in Proverbs 18:11, "*A rich man's wealth is his strong city, and like a high wall in his own imagination.*" The key word here is *imagination*. Their security in their *high wall* of wealth is just an illusion. But for them this security is a reality. Consequently, they see no danger, no trouble, no difficulty that their wealth cannot solve and/or protect them from.

The rich, young ruler blatantly manifested this attitude of personal security. He confidently came to Jesus not as a broken, desperate, searching, begging man looking to be rescued and brought to safety, but as a man who already felt quite secure. Jesus saw this attitude and cut right to the chase telling him to dispose of his security and become begging poor. Then and only then could he be eternally secure. Sadly, it was impossible for him.

Solomon makes it quite clear in Proverbs 11:28a that, *"He who trusts in his riches will fall."*

The insecurity of material possessions is the very reason Jesus told us, *"Do not store up for yourselves treasures on earth, where moth and rust destroy, and where thieves break in and steal. But store up for yourselves treasures in heaven, where moth and rust do not destroy, and where thieves do not break in and steal"* (Matthew 6:19-20 NIV).

David says it simply in Psalm 62:10, *"When riches increase, do not depend on them"* (GW).

It is impossible for a rich man to enter the Kingdom of God who still lives under the damning illusion that his material wealth somehow provides him any measure of personal security in this life or the next.

The Damning Illusion of *Personal Significance*

If it is all about me, it is impossible for it to be all about God. Wealth leads those who possess it to believe the damning illusion that their wealth has made them important—that they really are something. The world knows their name. The world acknowledges their success. The world shows them respect. They have come to believe, *"my power and the strength of my hand made me this wealth"* (Deuteronomy

8:17). They have grown quite in love with themselves and all their stuff.

They are full of themselves making it impossible for them to become full of God. Their throne is already occupied and there is no room for any competing monarchs. They live, think, and act like they are the center of their own universe — the ultimate narcissist. The rich person who cannot get *past* himself can never get *to* God.

It is impossible for a rich man to enter the Kingdom of God who still lives under the damning illusion that his wealth somehow gives him any measure of personal significance.

The Damning Illusion of *Personal Sovereignty*

"Nobody is going to tell me what to do. I have the gold. I'll make the rules. I am the captain of my own ship. I am the master of my own fate. I do not need anyone. I do not need anything."

Does this sound familiar? It sounds like the comments of the rich farmer in Luke 12:16-21,

> *The land of a rich man was very productive. And he began reasoning to himself, saying, "What shall I do, since I have no place to store my crops?" Then he said, "This is what I will do: I will tear down my barns and build larger ones, and there I will store all my grain and my goods. And I will say to my soul, 'Soul, you have many goods laid up for many years to come; take your ease, eat, drink and be merry.'" But God said to him, "You fool! This very night your soul is required of you; and now who will own what you have prepared?" So is the man who stores up treasure for himself, and is not rich toward God.*

The farmer foolishly believed, "I am set for life."

There is no more blatant statement of wealth's damning illusion of personal sovereignty than in Revelation 3:17, *"You say, 'I am rich; I have acquired wealth and do not need a thing.' But you do not realize that you are wretched, pitiful, poor, blind and naked"* (NIV). Wealth blinds its possessors to their true condition. They see themselves as rich and independent, when in reality they are destitute and helpless.

It is impossible for a rich man to enter the Kingdom of God who still lives under the damning illusion that his wealth somehow gives him any measure of personal sovereignty.

Jesus obviously knew that these damning illusions of wealth are so alluring, so deceiving, and so addictive that those who possess great wealth would be unwilling to ever trade in these damning illusions for what is true security, true identity, and true freedom in Christ. Until a person becomes *begging poor*, it is impossible for him or her to enter the Kingdom of God.

Let me close with a word of caution for those who have found the Kingdom of God and who have also been blessed to have accumulated a good bit of wealth. We must be careful to not allow ourselves to be seduced into embracing any of these damning illusions of wealth which would cripple our walk and destroy our witness.

We always need to remain *begging poor* regardless of what our balance sheet may tell us.

Some *Food for Thought* Questions

1. In what ways has your affluence hindered your relationship with Christ?
2. How comfortable do you feel seeing yourself as *begging poor*?
3. In what ways have you seen yourself attempting to be in charge of your own world?

Spiritual Thoughts on *Generosity*

Instruct those who are rich in this present world not to be conceited or to fix their hope on the uncertainty of riches, but on God, who richly supplies us with all things to enjoy. Instruct them to do good, to be rich in good works, to be generous and ready to share, storing up for themselves the treasure of a good foundation for the future, so that they may take hold of that which is life indeed.

1 Timothy 6:17-19

I want each of you to take plenty of time to think it over, and make up your own mind what you will give. That will protect you against sob stories and arm-twisting. God loves it when the giver delights in the giving.

2 Corinthians 9:7 THE MESSAGE

Day 8

Tithing: The Enemy of Generosity

The idea of tithing as the standard for acceptable giving has so permeated the church that very few (including pastors and elders) even question its validity or application to those of us who are living on this side of the cross. Many pastors and preachers emphasize tithing in hopes that their congregations will increase their giving above the national average of evangelicals, which is only about three percent. They believe that if they could get everyone in their congregation to start tithing, the church would have more money than it needed in order to do all that it wanted to do. Consequently, pastors fervently teach tithing as the *floor* at which every Christian ought to *start* their giving—the minimum entry point. I know of one church in my town that requires attendees to commit to tithing in order to become members. Pastors are not really aware that while their efforts to promote tithing might increase giving for a few, it actually ends up doing more harm than good to everyone in their congregation.

Let me illustrate. Take any congregation that is being consistently and regularly indoctrinated with tithing as the giving standard. Those who, for whatever reason—good or bad—are not able or willing to tithe are made to feel guilty that they are giving less than they "owe" God. So their giving is accompanied with feelings of guilt because they are told they are "robbing God." (See Malachi 3:8.)

Then you have those who are tithing to the penny. If they get a paycheck for $3,125.60, they will write a check to the church for $312.56. They are content to give exactly what they have been taught God has prescribed for them to give. Their giving will only increase as their income increases (mathematically to the penny).

Then there are those rare few who have broken over the tithe standard taught by the church and are now giving over ten percent. They often look upon themselves with some sense of pride because they are actually exceeding the required, minimum standard of giving.

Now let me ask you, which of these attitudes of giving is healthy—giving with guilt, giving legalistically to the penny, or giving with pride?

You see, as soon as you employ some mathematical formula to determine how much someone ought to be giving—to determine what God expects—you actually create spiritual, psychological, and emotional barriers to *generous giving*. We are all fallen, sinful creatures and consequently want to know what the "rules" are because we want to please God. How much church attendance, prayer time, scripture reading, giving, etc. will be enough to keep God happy with us? So, if we accept a formula for giving, we will use it as the predetermined acceptable standard and no longer feel any need to *seek out God's will for our personal giving*.

However, the New Testament never mentions tithing as the rule and standard for New Testament Christian giving—not even one verse. There is a very good reason for this. The New Testament calls Christians to give *by faith* (life) and not to give *by law* (death). (See Romans 8:2.) How much I decide to give of what the Lord has entrusted to me is just as intimately personal and individual as every other aspect of my Christian life.

To put this into perspective, let me ask:

- Has God prescribed how many minutes I must pray each day?
- Has He stipulated how many verses He expects me to read each week?
- Has He established how many people I am required to witness to each month?

The answer is an obvious "No" to all of them. God has prescribed none of these as His "acceptable standard" for being a "good Christian." Rather it is up to each of us individually to seek the Lord *by faith* and allow Him to direct us in how much of these activities we should be participating in.

Similarly, our giving is to be arrived at by careful, personal self-examination and seeking the Lord's direction in how much we should give as we evaluate this crucial area of financial stewardship. May I suggest that 2 Corinthians 9:7 gives us the Christian methodology for deciding how much we personally should be giving back to the Lord, not the scriptures of the Old Testament on tithing. Paul instructs, *"Each man should give what he has decided in his heart to give"* (NIV). In other words, the amount of our giving proceeds *from our heart*, not from our calculator. Our giving is to grow out of a personal relationship with Christ and not merely a prescriptive formula arrived at mathematically.

I can tell you with certainty that a poor woman who chooses to sacrificially give $500 out of her meager $12,000 annual Social Security income is being substantially more generous than the businessman who is giving $50,000 of his $350,000 annual income, even though the woman is giving only four percent and the businessman is giving fourteen percent.

Occasionally, I have been asked by affluent people, "How much should we be giving?" They sense that ten percent is no longer the right percentage for them and they are looking for someone to give them the appropriate percentage. My answer is always the same, "That is a very important question. Unfortunately, you are asking it of the wrong person. You need to ask that question to the One who owns all your stuff."

Many pastors I have talked with about generosity vs. tithing express the same gnawing concern. They fear that if they tell their congregation they are not required to tithe, the church's weekly offerings will collapse. I disagree. If believers were properly taught and really came to understand and live out the idea of *generous giving by faith* instead of *legalistic giving by math*, I believe that Christians' giving would explode. It may not happen overnight, because the church will have to overcome years of bad teaching, but once people really understand they need to go to their knees to decide how much to give instead of their calculators, we will likely see another outbreak of generosity that might compare to what the Israelites experienced in the construction of the Tabernacle. Their giving was so "over the top" Moses had to command them to stop giving. (See Exodus 35:20-36:7.)

I recently attended a meeting in which the speaker was enthusiastically telling about a financial advisor who had a wealthy client selling a $1.5 million asset, and the advisor had asked him about tithing on the sale price to the Kingdom, which he ended up doing. What struck me as unfortunate in this story is that the advisor did not ask his client if he personally needed any of the sale proceeds. Maybe he should have given one hundred percent of the sale proceeds to the Kingdom—and if not one hundred percent, how much might God want to use of these funds for His purposes? Possibly an even more challenging question for this client to ask himself would be, "How much of this $1.5 million would I have to give away for the gift to be a real, sacrificial act of faith on my part?"

The first option—the tithe—is clean, mathematically simple and requires little thought. The second—generosity—is neither clean nor simple and requires genuine soul searching, faith testing and "wrestling with God." In our struggle to find an amount right for giving each week, we might find ourselves feeling compelled to ask a similar question, "How much would I have to give to the Lord in order for my giving to be both generous and sacrificial?"

I hope you can see why I say that tithing is the enemy of generosity. If believers are ever going to become generous givers, we must first kill the legalistic, Old Testament doctrine of tithing and replace it with the New Testament directive of 2 Corinthians 9:7.

I would be remiss not to mention the "rest of the story" of 2 Corinthians 9:7 as well. Paul concludes this verse by giving us the emotional outcome of giving generously by faith vs. giving legalistically by math. He says, *"Each man should give what he has decided in his heart to give, not reluctantly or under compulsion, for God loves a cheerful giver"* (NIV). Giving legalistically according to a formula too often produces a reluctant giver who is giving out of compulsion. Giving generously by faith produces a cheerful giver who is giving out of overflowing joy. Paul says this giver is the one whom God loves. I personally opt for the latter. How about you?

Some *Food for Thought* Questions

1. How do you determine how much you will give?
2. Have you ever been motivated to give out of guilt or obligation? When and why?
3. How much joy do you really receive through your giving? Why is that?

Day 9

Who Sets the Limit on Your Giving?

Affluent Christian families have become so conditioned by the appeal of the IRS' "matching gift program" that many have unconsciously allowed the IRS to set the ceiling on their charitable giving—namely fifty percent of their Adjusted Gross Income (AGI). What I mean by "matching gift program" is that the IRS agrees that for every one dollar you give to support Kingdom causes, it will reimburse you forty percent of that gift (assuming a maximum tax bracket). So, for each dollar a family gives, they are giving sixty cents and the IRS is giving forty cents—a really nice deal! But this IRS' "matching gift program" only applies to gifts made up to fifty percent of your AGI. Anything you give beyond the fifty percent AGI limitation will not be matched by the IRS. Two critically important issues seem to emerge in this situation that I think need to be honestly and carefully considered—one of these issues is spiritual and the other is financial.

The Spiritual Issue

Who is setting the ceiling on your giving—God or the IRS? What if God wanted you to give away sixty percent of your AGI this year? Is there any biblical or spiritual basis upon which we should allow the taxing agency of our country to regulate how much we give? What if the IRS' "matching gift program" was reduced to twenty-five percent of your AGI next year, would you consequently reduce your maximum giving to only twenty-five percent? What if it went away altogether?

Do you see my point? If we genuinely believe that everything we possess belongs to the Lord, our primary question should be, "How much of what the Lord has entrusted to me does He want me to deploy this year, regardless of any limits set by the 'matching gift program' of the IRS?" Should we not be seeking God's criteria for how much we will give of what we have each year and not allowing the IRS to set the limit of our giving?

Might it be an uncomfortable conversation with the Lord if He were to ask us why we did not give away more of the surplus He entrusted to us than what the government would match? Might we respond, "Well, you know Lord, there was this fifty percent tax deduction limit on my AGI giving and I did not want to exceed that. You know, I wanted to be a good steward."

What if the Lord were to look at you and say, "If you were that concerned about being a good steward, why did you not more carefully explore *all* your giving options? There were strategies that would have allowed you to tax-efficiently give considerably more than you did, but you did not take advantage of them."

Unless God has clearly told you to set your limit of giving at fifty percent of your AGI, it might not be a good idea to get real comfortable with that ceiling as your chosen giving limit. Remember, *"Woe to those who are at ease in Zion"* (Amos 6:1).

The Financial Issue

What if I told you that with creative planning you could exceed fifty percent of your AGI in giving and still effectively participate in the IRS' "matching gift program?" And that you can use your current charitable giving to transfer your children's inheritance to them—gift/estate tax free? Would these possibilities pique your curiosity? Let me give you a simple scenario of how it might work.[1]

Jim and Barbara Brown have a net worth of approximately $30 million. Their AGI is consistently about $2 million annually. They both love the Lord and annually they give away just over $1 million (fifty percent of their AGI). They, like other generous Christians, have arbitrarily set a limit on their annual giving to be equal to fifty percent of the AGI in order to take full advantage of the IRS' "matching gift program." The Browns have three sons that are entering their real estate business. The Browns want to eventually turn over their entire real estate operation and holdings to their sons, but would face massive gift and/or estate taxes if and when they transfer their assets to the boys. They were open to giving more away annually, but also wanted to do it in the most tax effective way possible.

As part of a comprehensive Master Stewardship Plan, Jim and Barbara will place three of their commercial buildings (worth $7 million) into an Accelerated Inheritance Trust (AIT). The trust will donate its annual $500,000 income directly to their family foundation for Kingdom deployment. All this trust income now bypasses their AGI reducing it to $1.5 million. This means that their new deductible AGI giving limitation is now only $750,000. However, one hundred percent of the AIT trust income ($500,000) is going directly to their foundation bypassing their AGI giving limitation altogether. This integrated giving strategy increases the Brown's total, "tax deductible," annual giving to $1.25 million or sixty-three percent of their original AGI. Let me break it down for you in the following chart to see it more clearly:

---

[1] This illustration has been significantly simplified.

	Old Giving Plan	New Giving Plan
AGI	$2,000,000	$1,500,000
Fifty Percent AGI Giving	$1,000,000	$750,000
AIT Giving	$0	$500,000
Total Annual Giving	$1,000,000	$1,250,000
Percent of Giving	50%	63% [1]

What makes this strategy even sweeter is that after fifteen years, the Accelerated Inheritance Trust (AIT) will terminate and its $7 million of real estate holdings will pass to their three son's gift tax free, saving them over $3.5 million in transfer taxes and not using any of their lifetime exclusions.

Intelligent planning by the Browns (1.) increased their "tax deductible" giving over the next fifteen years by $3.75 million, (2.) passed $7 million in assets on to their sons, and (3.) eliminated the $3.5 million in gift taxes on the transfer. The Browns indeed viewed this as a win-win-win situation.

Jesus called us to be "*shrewd* (creative*) as serpents and as innocent* (honest) *as doves*" (Matthew 10:16). Jim and Barbara certainly were both creative and honest in managing and deploying what the Lord had entrusted to them. I think when they each stand before the Lord, they will no doubt hear, "Well done, good and faithful steward."

---

[1] 63% of original $2 million AGI

Some *Food for Thought* Questions

1. How has the IRS' "matching gift program" limitation influenced your total Kingdom giving?
2. If Kingdom giving would no longer be tax deductible would you continue giving as you are now? If not, what Kingdom causes would you stop supporting because of your reduced giving?
3. How creatively are you using the IRS' "matching gift program" to fully maximize your Kingdom giving?

Day 10

How Much Would You Give if You Knew Jesus was Coming Back Next Year?

How Much Would You Give if You Knew Jesus was Coming Back Next Year? I do not have any inside information here, but for the sake of discussion, what if we could somehow know that Jesus was indeed, coming back this time next year? It is certainly a question that should cause all of us to reflect. If your answer to this question is different than how much you are currently planning to give this coming year, it might be good to ask yourself, "Why?" Why would the amount you give this year be different if Jesus was coming back in one year instead of twenty years or one hundred years from now? There may be a number of reasons for why your giving would be higher and I think it might be good to contemplate some of those reasons.

Reason #1: With only one year left we would be willing to make much greater personal, material sacrifices since it would only be for one short year before we eternally relocate. In the grander scheme of eternity, twelve months is pretty insignificant.

I know when I exercise I am able to endure much greater physical "torture" because I know that my workout is only going to last forty-five minutes. We are usually far more willing to give something up for *Lent* than we are to give it up for *life*. Would this be true of our current giving practices?

Reason #2: With only one year left our giving amount might be different because our eternal perspective has changed. As the old hymn says, "the things of earth grow strangely dim in the light of His glory and grace." As the new heaven and the new earth get closer, this old one does not seem quite so attractive.

Think about the value of a confederate dollar in 1861, when the Civil War began, compared to the value of that dollar in March of 1865, a month before the war and the Confederacy came to an end. That confederate dollar after April of 1865 would be worthless to whoever held it. So, giving Confederate dollars away just before the end of the war was really not much of a gift. Likewise, as the return of Christ moves closer, the "things of earth" grow more and more worthless to us because it will not be a measure of anything of value in the next life.

That is what makes the picture of the streets in heaven being paved with gold so humorous. We take gold, which is universally valued here on earth, and God uses it as pavement in heaven. Jesus told us, "...*for that which is highly esteemed among men is detestable in the sight of God*" (Luke 16:15).

What the world values here is worthless there! Conversely, what the world considers worthless here is priceless there. Would this be true of our current giving practices?

Reason #3: Our personal giving would naturally increase because sending our financial resources on ahead would be more appealing since we would be getting a much larger reward when we get to heaven next year? (See Matthew 6:20, 19:21.)

Obvious, you cannot take it with you, but you can send it on ahead. If we knew that "ahead" would be only one year away and not decades or centuries away, we might view the temporal "loss" of our immediate enjoyment of and security in these things to be a quite compelling trade off. Would this be true of our current giving practices?

A Totally New Perspective

Something very interesting seems to happen to our viewpoint when we dramatically shorten the timeline. The world and our place in it are viewed from a totally new perspective, while the real priorities of life seem to literally explode within our consciousness. We find every area of our lives quickly reshuffled creating an entirely new order of priorities. And all too often these new life priorities do not include what currently consumes much of our daily list of "to dos." In life, the *tyranny of the urgent* is constantly seeking to override the *priority of the important*. We always seem to take time for the trivial and the unimportant, often because we mistakenly believe that there will always be time for getting to the "big stuff" later. Well, what if there was no "later"? What if there was no "next year"?

If we only had one more year to impact the world with what God has entrusted to us, would we be living and giving differently than we are planning to do this next year? If so, it might be a good spiritual and mental exercise to take some time to recalibrate our priorities to reflect an eternal mission instead of a temporal one—in the light of a shorter timeline rather than a longer one.

Some *Food for Thought* Questions

1. How would your giving change if you knew Jesus was coming back this time next year?
2. What is preventing you from giving an increased amount over the next year even if Jesus delays His coming?
3. What changes would you need to make in your life and lifestyle for your giving to be unaffected by the amount

of time you have left to impact the world before you eternally relocate or Christ returns?

Day 11

What is Your Most Valuable Possession?

What is your most valuable possession? When you first read this question your mind may quickly scroll through a balance sheet that lists all of your possessions, looking for your asset with the highest value. For most people, you hear their home is their most valuable asset, but for those whose net worth is substantial, that is seldom true. Instead, is it your business, one of your real estate holdings, or your investment portfolio? No matter which asset you may select as the most valuable, you will have picked the wrong one. Our materialistic culture drives us to think of our *things* when we think of our valuables, but there are other non-material things that are worth much more.

I would suggest to you that the correct answer to this question can be found by looking on a different balance sheet. Many years ago I heard Bob Buford, a self-made multimillionaire and author of the book *Halftime: Changing your Game Plan from Success to Significance*, speak at a conference. Right in the middle of the presentation he made a comment that was so profound and struck me so deeply that I do not think I really heard anything else he said for the rest of his presentation. He paused, gave a reflective look, and then commented, "It seems insane to me that a person would be willing to trade what he has a shortage of—time—in order to gain more of what he already has a surplus of—wealth." You cannot read this once and fully absorb it, so look at it again. "It seems insane to me that a person would be willing to trade what he has a shortage of—time—in order to gain more of what he already has a surplus of—wealth."

So, what is your most valuable asset? It is the time that you still have "banked" in this life. Your "time on this earth" account is all too quickly shrinking with every day that passes. And the most troubling part of this time account is that we cannot see how much we have left. Is it days, months, years, decades?

We often hear people ask the question, "How do you spend your time...?" This is a very accurate way to phrase how we use our time: we *spend* it. Unlike your financial accounts that you can make additional deposits into and build the account in the future, you can make no additional deposits into your time account. The total number of days allotted to us was deposited into our time account before we were even conceived. King David confirms this in Psalm 139:16, when he acknowledges, *"And in Your book were written all the days that were ordained for me, when as yet there was not one of them."* So, all of us will spend our time on something—and once it is spent, it is gone.

The truth of Bob Buford's comment is nowhere more clearly illustrated than in the story of the rich farmer we looked at earlier. After another excessive bumper crop season, he says,

This is what I will do: I will tear down my barns and build larger ones, and there I will store all my grain and my goods. And I will say to my soul, 'Soul, you have many goods laid up for many years to come; take your ease, eat, drink and be merry.' But God said to him, 'You fool! This very night your soul is required of you; and now who will own what you have prepared?'

Luke 12:18-20

How pathetically sad. He was willing to trade what he had almost nothing left of—time—in order to gain more of what he already had a surplus of—wealth. And then to add insult to his folly, God goes on to say of this man, *"So is the man who stores up treasure for himself, and is not rich toward God"* (Luke 12:21). He did not die rich—he died broke.

In Psalm 90:12, Moses asks God to help him use his time account wisely. He prays, *"So teach us to number our days, that we may present to You a heart of wisdom."* Paul said it this way in Ephesians 5:15-16, *"Therefore be careful how you walk, not as unwise men but as wise, making the most of your time, because the days are evil."* And not only are the days "evil," they are also very limited.

It seems to me that we need to manage our time account with even greater care than we manage our investment accounts. And we should be very leery about making any withdrawals out of our limited time account—"spending our time"—in order to make additional deposits into our already substantial—and temporal—investment accounts.

I have consistently heard from affluent Christian families their honest acknowledgment that they have a lot more money to give away than they have time. It is considerably easier for them to make a gift from their surplus wealth than it is to make a gift from their over-used and ever shrinking time account.

Keep this in mind: it is not in how much of our *wealth* we give; it is in how much of *ourselves* we give that allows us to fully experience the joy and blessing of giving. We have too much wealth in this country to experience much sacrificial giving from our material possessions. But we have precious little to give from our time account and that is where we learn to give like those who have little.

Wealthy families are beginning to catch the vision and see the power of short-term family mission trips to needy countries. Can you guess what proves to be the greatest obstacle in pulling off such a trip? It certainly is not the cost. That is the easiest part of the trip. The hardest part of the trip is finding the time for all of the members of the family to make the trip—to make a difference. The problem is time, not money.

When I was a young boy, I spent a good bit of time visiting my grandmother. She was a zealous and committed Christian woman and everywhere you turned in her small home, there were signs of her faith—a Bible on the coffee table—plaques and pictures on the walls—Bible verses on the refrigerator. There was one plaque in particular that made a significant impact on my thinking as a young boy. I did not realize it then, but I do now. The little plaque read, "Only one life 'twill soon be past, only what's done for Christ will last." My entire life, for the most part, has been one continuous effort to use the brief time that God has allotted me to do something that will have an eternal impact. Without this ultimate, eternal objective, life is correctly summed up by Solomon, "*All of it is meaningless, a chasing after the wind*" (Ecclesiastes 2:17 NIV).

What is your most valuable asset? How are you using your most valuable asset to do something that will last for eternity? Our cry should be, to paraphrase Isaiah 6:8, "Here I am Lord, [*spend*] me"

Some *Food for Thought* Questions

1. If someone were to be looking for evidence that you are a believer by looking at your calendar (how you spend your time), would they find sufficient evidence to confirm it? Why, or why not?
2. How did Bob Buford's comment strike you? How true is it of you?
3. How well are you managing your time account for eternity?

Day 12

The Greatest Gift You Have to Give

Have you ever wondered why a poor, old woman living in the slums of Calcutta, India, who devoted her life to the mundane task of caring for unwanted, starving children was internationally known and revered and even awarded the distinguished Nobel Peace Prize? What did she do to deserve such impressive notoriety? Who was this woman? You and the rest of the world knew her. She was Mother Teresa.

By our materialistic, American standards, Mother Teresa was a miserable failure. She never owned her own home. She had no money set aside for retirement, had not built a successful business or had much of an income. She did not own a car and wore the same style of clothes every day.

There was no reason why this fragile woman living in the inner city of an obscure, economically struggling country, working with hundreds of seemingly insignificant children should have earned such worldwide respect and prestigious accolades.

The fact is that as a country, specifically, and as a world, generally, we have drifted quite far from our original moral, ethical, and religious moorings. However, we have not drifted so far from them that we do not still deeply respect people who are willing to sacrificially give of themselves to help the helpless. Deep down, each of us knows that in so doing we will experience the highest level of personal fulfillment and spiritual joy even though this reality is seldom part of our daily consciousness. Sadly, we often find ourselves so busy in our headlong pursuit of living life that we actually end up missing the true essence of life.

It is not enough to simply read the biographies of great men and women who throughout history have happily traded a life of prosperity, luxury, and comfort for one of toil, sacrifice, disease, and even death to help those who cannot help themselves. You may be inspired by their great religious and humanitarian efforts, but you will never experience their tremendous blessing. They would all acknowledge that the fulfillment they found surpassed everything they voluntarily gave up in the trade.

A group of twelve youth and adults traveled to Juarez, Mexico to build a home for a needy family.

The husband of the family, for whom the group was to build the home, worked sixty hours each week to earn $30. Their current home was a tiny, one-room shanty constructed out of shipping skids and wrapped in tar paper. Their three-year-old daughter was an invalid and had major respiratory problems. She could only go outside for a few minutes at a time.

The campsite where the group pitched their tents was an old cow pasture located across the road from a pigpen. The restrooms were pit toilets where it seemed half the flies in all of Mexico resided. If the flies did not drive you out, the smell would. The other half of the flies in Mexico swarmed over their food as they tried to eat. They slept on the ground, and from about 2 AM on they were serenaded by a chorus of roosters making a sound night's sleep impossible. They cleaned up each day by pouring buckets of water over their heads. It was a challenging week for this group in many ways.

Yet, in spite of all of this, the group seized the challenge of building a humble dwelling for this needy family with the unity and zeal you might expect only from those who were building a grand palace for a king.

On the second day, as the team enthusiastically raised the walls to the new home, the mother stood by crying. All who saw her wept too. At that moment the group was reminded that they were not just building a house, they were helping people.

Seeing that woman's tears of joy made enduring all the discomfort of the trip wholly inconsequential. The group had again come to appreciate the words of Jesus, *"It is more blessed to give than to receive"* (Acts 20:35b). In this very small act of kindness, they had been reminded of this enduring truth.

What is interesting is that this group came home richer than they were before the trip. Some left their wives and children to go. Some took a week off work. They all spent money to go and they all endured physical discomfort. Yet, they came home richer. How? The answer cannot be explained in physical terms because it transcends the realm of the physical. It can only be explained in spiritual terms. And the explanation is this: *You will always make a profit, when you give yourself away to others.*

Let me suggest that the personal delight of giving massive sums of money away is decidedly minuscule in comparison to the joy you will realize by giving *yourself* away to a worthy cause.

The story of the rich young ruler expresses this truth perfectly. Jesus was not really interested in this young man's wealth. In fact, Jesus told him to give it all away to the poor. What Jesus really wanted was the *young man himself.*

What is the greatest charitable gift you have to give? *Yourself!* Why not make a gift of yourself to a worthy Kingdom cause? You will be all the richer for it.

Some *Food for Thought* Questions

1. How have you personally given of yourself for the good of others?
2. What would have to change in your life to enable you to give of yourself to others on a regular basis?
3. If your life continues as it is, what will people remember you for after you eternally relocate? How pleased will you be about that?

Day 13

How Does the Love of God Abide in Him?

Do you have a verse or two in the Bible that you rather wish was not in there? I think all of us do. Like, maybe, *"love your enemies"* (Matthew 5:44) or forgiving people *"seventy times seven"* (Matthew 18:22) or *"regard one another as more important than yourselves"* (Philippians 2:3)? These verses are like spiritual "thorns in the flesh" that continue to expose our lingering sinful, fleshly natures.

But there is another verse in the Bible that I also wish was not in there. And I expect when I share it with you, you might wish it gone too.

In the movie *The Wizard of Oz*, Dorothy, Scarecrow, Lion, and Tin Man are cowering before the Wizard. Dorothy's dog Toto runs over to a curtain and pulls it back exposing a mere man pretending to be the great and powerful wizard. Do you remember what this man said to all of them as they stood there staring at him in shock? Still trying to perpetuate the fraud, still acting the part of the Wizard, he yells out over the loud speaker, "Ignore that man behind the curtain!" Well, after reading this verse, it will be very difficult to "ignore the man behind the curtain." The jig will be up. The real you will be exposed. And if you are like me, when the curtain is pulled back, you will not at all like what others will see.

This troubling passage is found in 1 John 3:17 and it says (are you ready?), *"But whoever has the world's goods, and sees his brother in need and closes his heart against him, how does the love of God abide in him?"* Ouch!

"Whoever..." — Does whoever include me? Whoever?

"has the world's goods..." — Any goods? Does He mean surplus goods that I do not need or want — goods that if I gave them away would not affect my lifestyle? Or does this include worldly goods that I like and want to keep?

"and sees his brother..." — Any brother? Living anywhere in the world?

"in need..." — Any material need? Like hunger? Or thirst? Or nakedness? Or sickness? Or persecution?

"and closes his heart against him..." — You mean if I refuse to do something about his need?

"how does the love of God abide in him?" — Are you asking how does the love of God abide in *me*?

Do you mean that unless I use my material possessions to meet people's needs when I am aware of them, John is calling my love of God into question? I think it does. Ouch — no, double ouch!

Does this mean whenever I walk by a homeless person, I am supposed to respond to that need? What about when I see or hear about believers in other parts of the world who are suffering terribly? Is the love of God supposed to move me to do something about it with the worldly possessions I have at my disposal? When I hear about an orphan boy in Haiti who needs food, are you saying if the love of God is abiding in me, I will send him the $15 a month he needs?

Jesus said it this way,

"For I was hungry, and you gave Me something to eat; I was thirsty, and you gave Me something to drink; I was a stranger, and you invited Me in; naked, and you clothed Me; I was sick, and you visited Me; I was in prison, and you came to Me." Then the righteous will

answer Him, "Lord, when did we see You hungry, and feed You, or thirsty, and give You something to drink? And when did we see You a stranger, and invite You in, or naked, and clothe You? When did we see You sick, or in prison, and come to You?" The King will answer and say to them, "Truly I say to you, to the extent that you did it to one of these brothers of Mine, even the least of them, you did it to Me."

Matthew 25:35-40

Do you mean in a very real sense when I look into the face of a suffering and needy believer I am looking into the face of Christ? And if I were to help that needy person using my worldly goods, I am actually giving to Jesus? Proverbs 19:17 says, *"He who is kind to the poor lends to the Lord"* (NIV).

James 1:27 says, *"Pure and undefiled religion in the sight of our God and Father is this: to visit orphans and widows in their distress."* *"Pure religion"* is helping the helpless in their time of need. James goes on to ask in James 2:15-16, *"If a brother or sister is without clothing and in need of daily food, and one of you says to them, 'Go in peace, be warmed and be filled,' and yet you do not give them what is necessary for their body, what use is that?"*

Or still echoing in the background is John's piercing question, *"But whoever has the world's goods, and sees his brother in need and closes his heart against him, how does the love of God abide in him?"*

Is closing your heart against the poor as easy for you as it is for me? Are you able to see a need and in a matter of seconds, feel compassion and then almost instantly dismiss it with thoughts like, "Well, it is probably their own fault that they are in this mess anyway. They need to learn the hard lesson that God wants to teach them."

Or, "If I helped them out with some money, they would probably just use it for alcohol or drugs, but not for food. That would not be a good use of God's money."

Or, "The needs in that country are so massive that my little bit of money will not really make any difference—so why give anything?"

Or, my personal inclination, just look the other way and ignore them. The feelings of sadness and pity for the plight of the needy that might lead me to actually do something about their need, I have learned, will pass quite quickly if I just ignore them.

A family I know had allocated to each member of the family a certain sum of money to be used to meet the need of someone whose path they cross. As they were discussing what and how the help was going to be given, one of them spoke up and said, "You know just in the few minutes we have been discussing this, I have already come up with several ways to help." Other family members chimed in that they were thinking of ways to give too. Once you have a mindset that I have money to help and I want to get involved in making a difference in someone's life that has a need, the needs and the opportunities seem to appear at every turn.

What has changed? Were these needs not there before this meeting? No, the needs were there. What was not there was the mindset that, "*I am here on this earth to help those in need and I have some money set aside to do it with.*" It is a heart change that all of us need. For some of us with substantial wealth, we may need major heart surgery to extract ourselves from our tight grip on our possessions so that they can be used to impact the lives of people whom God has put in our path and graciously given us the funds to help.

Just try it. Allocate a certain sum of money—for example $10,000—and give yourself sixty days to find and meet the need of a person or people who the Lord brings into your life. You will learn a few things with this little exercise. One,

God will show you more needs than your $10,000 can meet. Two, you will be personally and deeply impacted by seeing the results in the lives of those who have been the beneficiaries of your kindness and generosity. Three, you will want to do it again. It is addictive! Start small and as God softens your heart and loosens your grip on your worldly possessions, your giving and need meeting efforts as well as your enthusiasm to give will grow.

After completing this giving exercise, get your Bible back out and re-read 1 John 3:17, *"But whoever has the world's goods, and sees his brother in need and closes his heart against him, how does the love of God abide in him?"* You will find that this verse no longer convicts and haunts you. It only affirms you and confirms your love for God. Now you can say, "I have the world's goods and I am constantly opening my heart and my hands to help my brothers in need and in so doing the love of God is manifested in my acts of love and kindness to those in need!"

If we have a surplus and know people who have a shortfall—and everyone that is reading this book does—when we start giving to meet those needs we will rejoice over the words of 1 John 3:17 instead of feeling condemned by them. And that is a much better way to feel about the Word of God and a much better way to live.

Some *Food for Thought* Questions

1. When was the last time you spontaneously gave money to someone who you saw in need?
2. If you had money specifically set aside to meet the needs of the poor, how might it change your attitude about helping the poor when you do see them?
3. Based upon 1 John 3:17, are you willing to make helping the poor a priority in your life and your giving?

.

Spiritual Thoughts on *Lifestyle*

Be very careful, then, how you live—not as unwise but as wise, making the most of every opportunity, because the days are evil. Therefore do not be foolish, but understand what the Lord's will is.

Ephesians 5:15-17 NIV

Keep the charge of the LORD your God, to walk in His ways, to keep His statutes, His commandments, His ordinances, and His testimonies, according to what is written in the law... that you may succeed in all that you do and wherever you turn.

Deuteronomy 6:17-18

Day 14

Are You Living Like a "Bucket" or a "Pipe"?

Are you living like a "bucket" or a "pipe"? This is a rather odd metaphorical question, is it not? Yet, it is only odd until you consider the purpose of a bucket and the purpose of a pipe. A bucket is designed to hold things (liquids, dirt, etc.). A pipe is designed to convey things through it (fluids, gases, etc.). The bucket holds what it receives and the pipe transfers on what it receives. So, in regards to the wealth that God has graciously entrusted to you, let me ask, "Are you living your life like a bucket or a pipe?" Are you holding on or passing on?

The Way of the Bucket

It is easy enough to live like a bucket and there are three reasons why we can indeed find ourselves living like a bucket.

#1: We can find ourselves living like a bucket when we ignore the ultimate end of all buckets.

I saw a bumper sticker some time ago that read, "He who dies with the most toys wins." I thought, "What an accurate way to express the world's view of life and possessions." But it immediately occurred to me that yes, this is true if the game of life is all about accumulation, but the sad tragedy is that he who dies with the most toys still dies and then someone else will get to play with all his toys.

David reminds us in Psalm 49:16-17 NIV,

> *Do not be overawed when a man grows rich* (when he has a big bucket and it is full)*, when the splendor of his house increases; for he will take nothing with him when he dies, his splendor will not descend with him.*

God condemns the rich farmer we discussed previously for this very thing: *"God said to him, 'You fool! This very night your soul is required of you; and now who will own what you have prepared* (what is left in your bucket)*? So is the man who stores up treasure for himself* (kept his own bucket full)*, and is not rich toward God"* (Luke 12:20-21).

What we keep in our bucket will eventually leak out, be stolen, taxed, evaporate, or spilled out when you "kick the bucket." This should give us reason to pause as we consider the folly of living life like a bucket.

#2: We can find ourselves living like a bucket when we bestow on ourselves "Most Important Person" status.

When what we want and need becomes the center of our attention, we will find ourselves living like a bucket. Jesus sternly warns us about the narcissistic attitude that we are the center of the universe. Again, the parable of the rich farmer is the classic example. The farmer was incredibly successful and had more than his current "bucket" could hold, so he chose to get rid of his smaller bucket and get a larger bucket so he could hold all the new stuff that he had accumulated. Jesus nails the selfishness of the farmer in Luke 12:15 when

94

He warns, *"Beware, and be on your guard against every form of greed; for not even when one has an abundance does his life consist of his possessions."*

The farmer's bucket was full and overflowing and he was proud of it, but God was not proud of him.

#3: We can find ourselves living like a bucket when we embrace the belief that filling our bucket is the way to find real happiness.

John D. Rockefeller honestly admitted, "I have made many millions, but they have brought me no happiness." However, we still want to believe the lie that "happy is the man whose bucket is full."

Henry Ford confessed after becoming a multi-millionaire, "I was happier doing a mechanic's job." Yet we still want to believe that "happy is the man whose bucket is full."

Solomon—who was perhaps the richest man to have ever lived—agonized about the futility of his riches in Ecclesiastes 2:11, *"When I surveyed all that my hands had done and what I had toiled to achieve, everything was meaningless, a chasing after the wind; nothing was gained under the sun"* (NIV). But we still want to believe that "happy is the man whose bucket is full."

Solomon observed in Ecclesiastes 5:13 what happens when people try to keep what is in their bucket for their own selfish enjoyment, *"I have seen a grievous evil under the sun: wealth hoarded to the harm of the owner"* (NIV).

The Way of the Pipe

I think we can agree that even though our sinful, fallen nature entices us to live life like we are a bucket, it is a cruel fantasy that ultimately leads to disappointment, destruction, and death. But what about living like a pipe? Let us consider this alternative.

#1: We will find ourselves living like a pipe when we understand God created us to be a pipe and not a bucket.

In God's economy, a pipe is infinitely more useful to Him than a bucket! He created us to be conduits and not receptacles of His blessings. In fact, let me ask you, "What happens if a pipe gets confused and starts thinking it is a bucket?" What is supposed to pass through gets stuck, becoming clogged and in need of being roto-rooted—so it can go back to doing what it was made to do—which is to let things flow *through* it, not just *to* it.

Do you know what happens to the body when its arteries get clogged up? Or, what a problem it is for the body when your colon gets clogged up? When your internal plumbing is not working, your body is going to be greatly hindered in its normal activities.

God has created many of us to be high-capacity pipes because he wants to pump huge amounts through us to support Kingdom causes worldwide. Let us look at what Paul tells Timothy in 1 Timothy 6:17-19,

Instruct those who are rich in this present world (high capacity pipes) *not to be conceited or to fix their hope on the uncertainty of riches, but on God, who richly supplies us with all things to enjoy. Instruct them to do good, to be rich in good works, to be generous and ready to share* (let it flow freely), *storing up for themselves the treasure of a good foundation for the future, so that they may take hold of that which is life indeed.*

Nothing produces "life indeed" like doing what God has created us to do. God has positioned us to turn on our spigot and let it flow!

As R. G. Letourneau said when asked how he could be giving ninety percent of his income away each year and yet still be getting richer. He smiled and confessed. "I keep shoveling it out and God keeps shoveling it right back in—and He has a bigger shovel!"

#2: We will find ourselves living like a pipe when we really believe that what we are letting flow through us today will ultimately flow back to us later.

This is the great eternal "payback" for being a pipe. The bucket gets what it gets while it is here and that is its reward. But the pipe receives a different payback. All that has flowed through it for all those years of life are being recorded and it will all be waiting for us when we relocate to our permanent residence. Malachi 3:16 says, *"A book of remembrance was written before Him for those who fear the Lord and who esteem His name."* God is monitoring your out-flow.

Jesus assures us of this eternal "payback" in multiple places. In Matthew 6:20-21, He encourages us, *"But store up for yourselves treasures in heaven, where neither moth nor rust destroys, and where thieves do not break in or steal; for where your treasure is, there your heart will be also."* We lay up for ourselves treasures in heaven by what we willingly divest ourselves of in giving to others *in this life.*

And again as we saw in Matthew 19:21, Jesus charged the rich, young ruler, *"If you wish to be complete, go and sell your possessions and give to the poor, and you will have treasure in heaven; and come, follow Me."* Pass it through now and it will be waiting for you in heaven. Jesus was not asking him to give it up; he was just asking him to send it on ahead for later use and enjoyment. Not a bad deal if we keep in mind that this life may last eighty years and eternity, well, it is a lot longer than that!

#3: We will find ourselves living like a pipe when the desires of God's heart truly become the desires of our heart.

Psalm 37:4 is a very powerful verse, *"Delight yourself in the Lord; And He will give you the desires of your heart."*

Most people have incorrectly interpreted this verse to say, "You delight yourself in the Lord and then the Lord will give you what you want," but it more accurately should be understood this way: "Delight yourself in the Lord and then the Lord will *give you His desires* for your heart." In other words, as we delight ourselves in Him, He will replace our heart's desires with His heart's desires, so that we will love what He loves and we will hate what He hates. That way we will have compassion on whom He has compassion.

And once God has our heart's desires aligned with His heart's desires, we will find ourselves driven to be a high-capacity pipe allowing as much grace and blessing as possible to fall upon those whom the Lord wants to touch and care for.

We must not forget the sobering words of our Lord who said, *"From everyone who has been given much* (high-flow capacity), *much* (high-flow capacity) *will be required"* (Luke 12:48b).

Jim Elliot, who was martyred trying to share Christ with a native tribe in South America, wrote, "He is no fool who gives what he cannot keep, to gain what he cannot lose." What we accumulate on this earth we cannot keep and what we accumulate in heaven we cannot lose. Seems like a "no brainer," does it not?

May I encourage those of you who God has blessed to be high-capacity pipes to freely open your spigot and let

God's blessings and provision pour forth on those who need a blessing from God! If we do, we will have everything to gain and nothing to lose.

Some *Food for Thought* Questions

1. When you reflect on your life, do you see more similarities to living like a bucket or living like a pipe?
2. Is there a disconnect between what Jim Elliott said ("He is no fool who gives what he cannot keep, to gain what he cannot lose.") and how you live?
3. In what ways are you like the rich, young ruler?

Day 15

Getting *Spiritually* Comfortable
with Your Wealth

"We're just regular people. We do not see ourselves as rich at all." I have been hearing this kind of comment from wealthy Christians for many years. I find it fascinating that when affluent people evaluate whether they are rich or not, they always do so by comparing themselves to people who are richer than they are. I suppose in using this method of evaluation no one in America is actually rich except for Bill Gates (the founder of Microsoft).

A number of years ago I worked with a man worth about $15 million. He wanted to introduce me to his friend who was worth about $150 million. I will never forget what he said to me about his friend. He said, "Compared to him, I'm small potatoes." I could not help but think, "Compared to 99.9 percent of the world a $15 million net worth is not *small* potatoes, it is *humongous* potatoes." However, "small potatoes" was his assessment because he was not comparing himself to the 99.9 percent, he was comparing himself to the .1 percent.

We recently hosted a conference and invited twelve wealthy Christian couples to attend. It was fascinating to see how many of them, when invited, either initially hesitated or somewhat resisted attending because they said they did not really see themselves as rich and thought they might feel uncomfortable being in a group of rich people. It was all I could do to keep from laughing out loud because, even though every one of these people are all rich by any measure, they are just as common and ordinary as every day house slippers. Many wealthy families simply do not feel entirely comfortable with the idea that they are rich. Most rich people, I have observed, are just ordinary people who have been extraordinarily successful at one thing.

What typically happens with these "salt of the earth" people who slowly and surely grow materially rich is that the spiritual, social, and strategic aspects of their wealth have not grown at the same pace as their ever-increasing net worth. This leaves them not quite believing they are rich and not exactly sure how to fully embrace or successfully relate to this "new found" material wealth, much less have real clarity on what God wants them to do with all of it. Consequently, these rich Christians most often end up substantially under-utilizing all their God-given resources because they are, in a very real sense, living a life that is contradictory to the current reality of their present material circumstances.

So, when I say "getting comfortable with my wealth," I do not mean that in so doing we should throw frugality to the wind and start spending money like there is no tomorrow. I also do not mean that we should develop some sense of pride because of all the riches we have accumulated. Nor do I mean that we should start putting our trust and confidence in the "provided" instead of the Provider. All three of these attitudes and actions are sinful responses to wealth and are a clear violation of scripture.

What I *do* mean when I say "getting comfortable with my wealth" is this.

(1.) We stop emotionally resisting that we are, in fact, rich.

(2.) We stop feeling some degree of embarrassment or guilt because we are rich while so many others in the world are poor.

(3.) We happily and humbly embrace the honor and the responsibility that accompanies being one of the relatively few who have walked on this planet that have actually become rich.

When we finally become properly comfortable with our wealth we will not flaunt it, but neither will we try to hide it. We will not waste it, but neither will we hoard it. We will not love it, but neither will we hate it. We will not deny it, but neither will we ignore it.

Instead, I want to address the three under-developed aspects of material wealth that commonly hinder rich Christians from fully maximizing their life-capacity and achieving the greatest possible Kingdom impact with all they are and have. We will consider these in the next three days.

Getting *Spiritually* Comfortable with Your Wealth

Wealthy Christians need to get *spiritually* comfortable with their wealth, especially since much of the Christian world looks at wealthy believers with a rather jaundiced eye. I think there are three primary obstacles that we need to break through in order to achieve a spiritual comfort with being wealthy.

Obstacle #1: Getting Past the Guilt of Wealth

There is clearly a stigma in religious circles towards Christians who are rich. It is more covert than overt, but it is there nonetheless. Anyone with wealth has felt it. It is an attitude that believes there is something spiritually questionable, at best, about any believer who is wealthy.

The Catholic Church has overtly promoted this mindset for centuries. Priests, monks, and nuns as a sign of their devotion to the Lord take vows of poverty. If they have any material possessions at the time they make this vow, they divest themselves of it all. Consequently, poverty became the model of total devotion to the Lord. So, where does that put a person who finds himself quite rich? They obviously must be materialistic and unspiritual, right?

Many think committed Christians should not be rich because if they were really serious about their relationship with the Lord they would give all their money away and become poor like Jesus. By the very fact that a person has wealth they are viewed as carnal Christians.

Another historical attitude that comes into play is the distinction between what is *secular* and what is *sacred.* Prayer, worship, Bible reading, meditation, and service are sacred activities (good), while work and making money are secular activities (bad). We have all heard the term "filthy lucre." Many believe that material things are secular and "dirty."

Martin Luther and John Calvin among others, made a great effort to debunk this false distinction between sacred and secular by teaching that everything a believer does is sacred—including work. The apostle Paul said it this way, *"Whatever you do, do your work heartily, as for the Lord"* (Colossians 3:23). Here are three assumptions that are commonly held within the Christian community that we need to evaluate.

Assumption #1: *Wealthy people are characteristically unscrupulous and dishonest.* There is an attitude that no one could have made any kind of wealth without having done something unethical, illegal, or immoral along the way to get them where they are now. They must have taken advantage of someone to have become as rich as they are—what I call the "Zacchaeus syndrome."

Assumption #2: *Wealthy people are characteristically greedy and materialistic*. People think that the wealthy's focus is on accumulating worldly and material things and they will make whatever sacrifice is necessary to gain greater riches. They already have more wealth than they could ever need and yet they are still working hard and getting richer—what I call the "Ebenezer Scrooge syndrome."

Assumption #3: *Wealthy people are characteristically selfish and narcissistic*. Many would suggest that with all the problems in the world, the rich actually give very little away to help all those in need. Look how much they have and how little of it is used to help others. It is all about them—what I call the "rich, young ruler syndrome."

If any of these three "assumptions" is actually true of us, in whole or in part, I think we need to come clean with the Owner, repent, and make things right. If these are not true of us, we need to set aside that nagging sense of guilt (self-imposed or other-imposed) for being rich and see it as a gift to be used for God's eternal purposes. Being affluent is nothing to be proud of, but neither is it anything to feel guilty about.

The Bible is full of followers of God who were rich: Job, Abraham, David, Solomon, Joseph of Arimathea, and Barnabas just to name a few. The Bible nowhere speaks negatively of these men because they possessed great wealth. If God is not condemning you for possessing wealth, why should you or others set a standard of judgment that even God has not imposed?

Obstacle #2: Getting Past the Myth of Tithing

As we have already discussed, one of the greatest hindrances to wealthy families getting comfortable with their wealth is the pervasive false teaching in the church about tithing. We have all been "drilled" for years in our churches with the directive that ten percent is the amount we "owe" God. To do less than ten percent is stealing from God.

Dr. Andreas Köstenberger and Dr. David Croteau responded to this subject by writing an exhaustive and scholarly research paper entitled, *Will a Man Rob God? (Malachi 3:8): A Study of Tithing in the Old and New Testaments* in which they consider every verse in the entire Bible that refers to tithing. Through it, they entirely debunk the notion that tithing is the biblical standard of giving for the New Testament church.[2]

As we discussed before, I believe that the New Testament guideline for giving can be found in 2 Corinthians 9:7, *"Each man should give what he has decided in his heart to give, not reluctantly or under compulsion, for God loves a cheerful giver"* (NIV). For some believers, giving two percent may demonstrate a real act of faith on their part, while others giving anything less than ninety percent of their income would require no faith. The New Testament standard for giving is to give as God directs, not according to a formula, and it requires each man to individually "examine himself" and give according to what the Lord lays on his individual heart as his personal expression of his love, gratitude, and worship to God. Keep in mind *"From everyone who has been given much, much will be required"* (Luke 12:48b).

When I raise this issue of giving by faith and not by math, people frequently object by telling me stories of people who were giving very little, if anything and then decided to begin tithing and immediately God started blessing them. I point out that I believe the reason God started blessing them was not because there was something magical about the percentage they decided to give, but because of the degree of faith they

---

[2] If you would like a copy of this research paper, please email me at jlink@kardiaplanning.com.

exercised in making the commitment to start giving sacrificially. I wonder if these new tithers would have only decided to give 9.75 percent instead of ten percent if nothing amazing would have happened in their lives. I think not. They were blessed because they exercised their faith, not because they complied with some prescribed, mathematical formula.

We must spiritually break through this myth of tithing so we can happily stand before the Owner of all our possessions and ask, "God, what do You want me to do with *all* Your stuff that I am holding for You? If You want it all, it is Yours. Just tell me where to send it." I think we would all admit that standing before God making this statement could be a very scary place to be—which leads us to our final obstacle.

Obstacle #3: Getting Past the Fear of Loss

There is absolutely no doubt that the single greatest obstacle to fully engaging the totality of a family's wealth in Kingdom initiatives (directly or indirectly) is the fear of loss. This fear of loss is incredibly pervasive among all who are affluent, both believers and unbelievers.

They simply fear that something might happen that would put them back to "square one" needing to start all over again. One wealthy gentleman repeatedly told me that he was retired and he did not want to do anything that might force him to have to go back to work again—a fear of loss. I asked one elderly lady many years ago, "How much would it take for you to feel like you would have enough to feel safe?" She looked at me and said without a moment's hesitation, "Honey, I will never have enough to feel safe"—a fear of loss. So, like Linus in Charlie Brown, we often cling to our wealth as some sort of a security blanket that we believe will somehow keep us safe. Yet, Solomon tells us the folly of this thinking in Proverbs 18:11, "*A rich man's wealth is his strong city, and like a high wall in his own imagination.*" Did you see what he said, "*in his own imagination?*" Finding any security in riches is merely a figment of our imagination.

If we are putting our faith in our wealth, we are facing a spiritual obstacle that will prevent us from fully living by faith and trusting in the Owner of the stuff we manage. I am ever encouraged in this very matter by David's observation in Psalm 37:25, "*I have been young and now I am old, yet I have not seen the righteous forsaken or his descendants begging bread.*" Our security is not in the provided—it is in the Provider.

Fear of loss is incompatible with faith. If you fear, you do not have faith. If you have faith you will not fear. Almost one hundred times from Genesis to Revelation, the Bible tells us to "fear not"—because faith is the spiritual antidote to fear.

Let me ask a very sobering question. If Jesus commanded you to do the same thing He commanded the rich, young ruler: "*If you wish to be complete, go and sell your posses- sions and give to the poor, and you will have treasure in heaven; and come, follow Me*" (Matthew 19:21). How would you respond? Would you react better than the rich, young ruler? The rich, young ruler was comfortable with his station in life and he was not willing to let Jesus take him down what appeared to him to be a significantly less desirable path.

I think what prevented this young man from obeying Jesus was his fear of loss. I think he stopped listening when Jesus told him to "give it all away" and he never heard the rest of Jesus' statement, "*...and you will have treasures in heaven.*" He was unwilling to give up temporal gratification and security in exchange for eternal gratification and secu- rity—in the long view, not a very wise decision.

When we can break through our fear of loss, we will be able to see what we possess from a totally different perspec- tive. Now, instead of our wealth being a source of great secu- rity, it becomes a source of great opportunity.

God wants us to get spiritually comfortable with His gift of riches. He wants us to rejoice in having it and be excited about using all of it to honor and glorify Him.

There is no place in God's purposes for us to feel guilty about being rich. We must (1.) jettison the myth of tithing as the acceptable standard of giving for Christians and (2.) develop a deeper and stronger faith in our Father's care and provision to help us overcome that gnawing fear of loss that can paralyze us from hearing and responding to the directives of our Father.

Look in a mirror and say this to yourself: "I am rich! God has given me the gifts I needed to become rich. I have faithfully used those gifts. He has blessed me with riches! God has a divine purpose for why He has made me rich. I intend to fully discover that divine purpose. I will fulfill that purpose the best I can for the rest of my life and beyond!"

What an honor and a noble, spiritual calling to be one of the few in all of human history to be trusted with riches. It is a great privilege and a great responsibility. Rejoice and be glad in it!

Some *Food for Thought* Questions

1. Have you ever felt guilty about having so much when other people have so little? Where is this guilt coming from?

2. How has the Old Testament teaching on tithing affected your level and measure of generosity?

3. How much do you struggle with the fear of losing what you have accumulated? Why?

Day 16

Getting *Socially* Comfortable with Your Wealth

One of the most surprising consequences of becoming wealthy is that your circle of close friends shrinks significantly. Increasing wealth often negatively affects a wealthy couple's ability to have meaningful relationships with people of ordinary means.

I recall an incident many years ago with a family while we were discussing their relationships with other people. In the middle of our discussion, the husband mentally left our conversation and started staring off into space. In a matter of seconds, tears began to fill his eyes. We all sat there in motionless silence. After waiting for a short time, I queried him about what he was thinking. He was so emotionally overcome by his thoughts that he was unable to respond. After a couple of minutes, he regained his composure, looked at his wife, and began trying to articulate what had moved him so. We just sat and listened.

He shared, "Honey, do you remember when we were young and just getting started in business—back when we did not have anything? At that time we had many close friends in church and in town. We were always doing things with other couples and other families. We were going over to their houses and they were coming over to ours. But as we have been talking it just hit me for the first time that the richer and more successful we have become over the years, the fewer close friends we have had—until finally today, I can honestly say, we really do not have any close, intimate relationships." As they became materially richer, they became relationally poorer.

Being much younger and much less experienced in working with wealthy families at that time, I was completely surprised by his revelation. I decided to do more research to see if this situation was unique to this couple or common to all wealthy couples. As I discussed this matter of relational isolation with other wealthy people and read what other professionals had written on the subject, I discovered that this was indeed the rule and not the exception among the wealthy. Hence, I learned that the old idiom, "It is lonely at the top" is indeed true for those who are at the top of the economic "food chain."

More recently, I had an opportunity to meet with another affluent couple. The couple was older and they lived in a very modest home (only about 1,200 square feet). Two older, American-made cars sat in their driveway. All signs would indicate this couple had very little. Yet, the college President that introduced us assured me they were extremely wealthy.

I entered their modest home and began a pleasant conversation with the couple. I learned that the wife was actually the husband's second wife. His first wife had died years earlier and they had now been married for over ten years.

His second wife had very little material possessions when she married her new husband who owned a substantial regional bank. Since marrying, they had done everything they possibly could to hide their wealth for fear that if her friends found out how wealthy they were, she would lose them. So they lived in a small home, drove older cars, shopped at Wal-Mart, and avoided doing things or having things that would give any appearance of them being wealthy.

Yet, with all their overt efforts to try to appear to be common, everyday people, their cover-up was futile. She shared that one day she and some of her girl friends were talking about going shopping and she said she did not know if she had enough money to go shopping at this nicer clothing store with her friends. One of her friends looked her in the eyes and said incredulously, "Martha, you are married to George. You can buy the store if you want to!" She was devastated. Her friends knew they were rich. In fact, everyone knew. Their extreme attempts to hide their wealth were both silly and sad, but their motivation for doing so was anything but silly and sad. They knew that wealth separates the "Haves" from the "Have Nots." Since she did not want to lose her "Have Not" friends, she tried to appear to be a "Have Not" herself.

Whenever I recall this story I am always reminded of what Solomon said in Proverbs 13:7, "*There is one who pretends to be rich, but has nothing; another pretends to be poor, but has great wealth.*" So often in America we see that those who are not rich want to live like they are, and those who are rich often want to live like they are not.

Many may think that the cause of this relational isolation is actually perpetrated by the wealthy who are ready to abandon relationships with whom it is no longer "socially appropriate" to associate. However, I would suggest that just the opposite is true. It is the common people who separate themselves from the wealthy.

As a family's wealth increases it becomes harder and harder to maintain relationships with people of average income. Barriers to meaningful relationships begin manifesting themselves, which prevent affluent families and families of ordinary means from maintaining or developing close and intimate relationships.

There are five common barriers that prevent wealthy people from maintaining meaningful relationships with more common people. Let me explain them briefly.

1. Wealthism

Wealthism is a prejudice that common people have towards those who are wealthy. Common people think, "If I had all the success and prosperity that you have, you would never hear me complain about anything! In fact, how can anyone who has as much stuff as you do possibly have any serious problems?"

You see, common people have bought into the false notion that wealth makes you happy and the more wealth you have, the happier you should be. They cannot imagine how anyone can have so much wealth and be unhappy about anything? This attitude is, of course, completely false, as those of you with wealth know. Not only do wealthy people endure many of the same kinds of problems other people do, there is also a rather long list of additional problems and challenges wealth presents that ordinary people have no idea about. Common people only focus on the benefits of possessing wealth and are oblivious to its burdens.

2. Wealth Intimidates

The sad truth is that common people are intimidated by wealth. Those who possess wealth can become larger than life, rather like movie stars and athletes. The average person is not able to enter into a real and meaningful relationship with these "celebrities," because they are "star-struck." They are much more inclined to ask for their autograph than ask them how their family is doing! Wealth places its holders in a "superstar" category and removes them from the masses who are awed by their success, their wealth, and their power.

3. Wealth Creates One-sided Relationships

This is a very interesting dynamic that for the most part positions the wealthy person as the giver and the common person as the receiver, sort of like parents and children. The simplest example of this reality is when they go out to lunch together. The wealthy person feels an obligation to pay for lunch because he can easily afford to and the common person has an unspoken expectation that the wealthy person will pay. Wealth creates these kinds of one-sided relationships that can be neither healthy nor long lasting.

4. Wealth Bestows Power

You have heard the old saying, "He who has the gold makes the rules." That is true and everyone understands this reality. So, it is extremely difficult for a common person to become an equal in any meaningful way with a wealthy person, because of the power his/her wealth provides.

5. Wealth Needs to Be Protected

It is necessary to protect wealth from those who would try to relieve its owners of it, either legally or illegally. Therefore, wealthy people build walls around their stuff and themselves to protect what they have from being taken. They buy locks to protect their "stuff." This is not only true physically; it is also true emotionally, because everyone is trying to "get into their pockets" for something. I knew a gentleman who wanted to pick the brain of a wealthy gentleman in his church about how to best invest in real estate. He knew this man had great experience in this area. When he asked this wealthy man if they could go to lunch together to talk, the wealthy man asked him, "What are you selling?" How sad, but true. Wealthy people are being "hit" on by everyone—

ministries, investment advisors, needy people, etc. This creates a significant barrier to healthy relationships when the "Haves" always find themselves questioning the "Have Nots'" motives for why they want into their life.

The key to overcoming these barriers and being able to enjoy meaningful relationships with less affluent people requires you to learn to build bridges instead of walls. In chapter sixteen of my book, *Family Wealth Counseling: Getting to the Heart of the Matter*, I share several stories of what some wealthy families have done to overcome the isolation that wealth routinely creates. Their creative approaches allow them to enjoy rich, wholesome, and intimate relationships with the other 99.9 percent of the world. In choosing to build bridges instead of walls, you will indeed become socially comfortable with your wealth and be both blessed and a blessing to those whose lives you are now able to genuinely touch.

Some *Food for Thought* Questions

1. How many close friends do you have right now? Are you happy with that number?
2. Do you ever try to hide your wealth from others? Why?
3. What are you doing to break down the barriers between yourself and the everyday people whose paths you cross each day?

Day 17

Getting *Strategically* Comfortable with Your Wealth

Over the past three decades, I have seen one universal reality that has been consistent. Of the hundreds of wealthy families I have spoken to, visited, and worked with, not one had come anywhere close to developing a comprehensive master plan to strategically maximize their resources. In fact, I would add that the wealthier the family is, the more inadequate their strategic planning has been.

Failure #1: Tax Planning

The most common example of this failure can be seen in how families arrange (or do not arrange) their finances to minimize or eliminate unnecessary income, capital gains, and estate taxes. Needless to say, this is not because they want to pay these taxes—they, of course, would rather avoid them. However, by not fully acknowledging the reality of the substantial wealth they now manage for the Lord, their tax exposure grows exponentially. When families see how much of their accumulated wealth and income they are going to lose to *optional* taxes, they are shocked and dismayed. This is just one reason why wealthy Christians need to get *strategically* comfortable with their wealth—so they can think and plan like people who have major tax issues and major tax planning opportunities rather than living in denial.

Failure #2: Inheritance Planning

Another example of the need to get strategically comfortable with their wealth is in regards to their heirs' inheritances. It is almost universally true that when the parents see what their current plan is going to do in regards to the size and timing of their children's/ grandchildren's inheritance, they are most often quite stunned.

Recently, parents saw illustrated that their current plan had their four children getting $34 million and their grandchildren were getting $17 million. They were both astonished and alarmed. They stared at their current plan flowchart in disbelief. They only wanted each of their four children to get $400,000 (a total of $1.6 million) and they did not feel compelled to give anything to their grandchildren—they felt that was their children's responsibility. How could their current plan be so far from their desires? It is really quite simple. Their wealth continued to grow to the point that what might have been a good plan years earlier was now a "disaster waiting to happen."

Over the years, I have also seen a number of families who, with the best of intentions when they were not so prosperous, set up trusts for their children and put some modest amount of their assets/businesses into these trusts. Some years later they discovered—to their shock and amazement—that these relatively small assets had skyrocketed in value and they had inadvertently made their children multimillionaires with enormous tax implications—something they never intended to happen. These situations are examples of how all too often the tax planning "tail" ends up wagging the family planning "dog."

Failure #3: Kingdom Giving

Lastly, failure to get strategically comfortable with your wealth will lead you to give substantially less to the Kingdom than you could or even should be giving. I find it particularly interesting to note that even with committed Christian families, their existing estate plans very seldom have made provision to give any of their accumulated wealth to support Kingdom initiatives. There is no doubt these families are open and happy to give to support the Lord's work, but because they have never become strategically comfortable with their wealth, they do not give any substantial amounts away during their lifetime or after they "relocate." So, they often inadvertently end up giving too much to the government, more than they think is wise to their heirs, and too little to the Kingdom.

However, once these wealthy couples recognized the need to do strategic, comprehensive, stewardship planning, they are able to implement plans that produce such powerful outcomes that even they are amazed at what they have done with what they have.

Let me illustrate the potential Kingdom impact if all affluent Christian families were to start planning with a Kingdom focus. With only fifteen families who have implemented strategic Master Stewardship Plans they have collectively eliminated over $290 million in taxes (income, capital gains, and estate taxes), ensured that they will have all they need to live on for the rest of their lives, set the children's inheritances at levels that are both well thought out and appropriate, and have released for deployment over *$500 million* in new, Kingdom giving.

If you do not think of yourself as being wealthy, you probably will not be willing to spend the time or money necessary to do the needed strategic planning that wealthy families can do to maximize the leverage of their wealth for the good of all concerned. Once you get comfortable with your wealth, you will find great excitement and a compelling fulfillment in the honor and privilege of being rich as well as appropriately thinking and acting like you are rich.

God granted you wealth for a purpose. You will only fully discover that purpose as you get spiritually, socially, and strategically comfortable with the reality that you are indeed wealthy. It is your responsibility as a child of God to come to grips with what Jesus told us: *"to whom much is given, much shall be required. From everyone who has been given much, much will be required"* (Luke 12:48).

Some *Food for Thought* Questions

1. How does your lack of acceptance of your level of wealth prevent you from being more strategic in using your wealth to its greatest Kingdom potential?
2. How can acknowledging that you really have the wealth you do, empower you to do even greater things for the Kingdom?
3. What has God given you this wealth for?

Spiritual Thoughts on *Purpose*

But I have raised you up for this very purpose, that I might show you my power and that my name might be proclaimed in all the earth.

Exodus 9:16 NIV

With this in mind, we constantly pray for you, that our God may count you worthy of his calling, and that by his power he may fulfill every good purpose of yours and every act prompted by your faith.

2 Thessalonians 1:11 NIV

Day 18

Are You Living Your Life on Purpose or by Accident?

To develop a thoughtful and effective Master Stewardship Plan, a couple really needs to begin the process by getting away as a couple for what I call a *Discovery Retreat*. We developed a *Life on Purpose Questionnaire* to guide couples in their discussions on the retreat. People have often asked why I call it a "Life on Purpose" Questionnaire. My answer is simple. You can choose to live your life one of two ways: you can either live your life *on purpose*, or you can live your life *by accident*. In other words, you can plan your life and live your plan, or you can simply let the flow of life events and circumstances sweep you down the river of time taking you wherever it will. The latter, sadly, is the way most people live their lives—by accident. The former is how God created us to live—on purpose. (See Ephesians 5:15-16, Psalm 90:12.)

Some might claim that there is something unspiritual about making plans, but for those of us who do, we are in good company. God made plans. (See Hebrews 11:40a, Jeremiah 29:11, Ephesians 1:11.) Paul made plans. (See 2 Corinthians 1:15-17, Romans 15:24.) And we are encouraged to make plans. (See Proverbs 16:3, 20:18, 21:5.)

Unfortunately, when it comes to building one's financial "empire" we can often find ourselves doing it without any real divine purpose behind it. Successful people continue to build up their "pile of stuff" because they have become exceedingly good at what they do. They also find great emotional enjoyment and personal satisfaction in building, so they keep on building without ever giving much thought to where it will end up.

However, I think there is a foundational question that we, as believers, need to ask ourselves, "What is my purpose for continuing to build my financial empire when my pile of stuff is already higher than I will ever need it to be?" Jesus tells us plainly that accumulating excess wealth as a sole end in itself is entirely futile. Jesus states, *"For what will it profit a man if he gains the whole world and forfeits his soul?"* (Matthew 16:26). For those who do this they are like the rich farmer who planned to tear down his smaller barns and build bigger barns to hold his surplus wealth. Remember, Jesus called him a *fool*.

There is no greater example of the utter folly of building without a purpose than the story of Sarah Winchester. Sarah was the wife of William Winchester, the only son of Oliver Winchester, the founder and owner of the Winchester Repeating Arms Company. Sarah and William had a daughter who died shortly after birth in 1866. This was followed by the death of her father-in-law (1880) and then her husband just a few months later (1881), leaving her with a fifty percent ownership in the company and an income of $1,000 a day (about $21,000 a day in 2008 dollars).

Sarah believed that her family was under some kind of a curse and consulted a medium to determine what she should do. The medium told her that her family was indeed cursed by the spirits of all the people that the Winchester rifle had killed. She should move out west and build a house for herself and all the tormented spirits who suffered because of her family. The medium also told her that if construction on this house were to ever cease, she would immediately die.

In 1884 Sarah moved to California and began one of the most bizarre building stories in American history. She began spending her $20 million inheritance and regular income to buy and begin renovating an eight-room farmhouse in what is now San Jose, California. From that day forward construction continued nonstop, twenty-four hours a day, seven days a week until Sarah's death at age eighty-three — a total of thirty-eight years. She kept no less than twenty-two carpenters busy continuously. The sounds of hammers and saws could be heard throughout the day and night for almost four decades.

At its zenith, this seven story house contained 160 rooms, forty bedrooms, forty-seven fireplaces, seventeen chimneys, and 10,000 windowpanes. What made Sarah's lifetime building project so bizarre was that it had no discernable architectural purpose or plan behind it. Closet doors opened to solid walls. Windows were in the floor. Stairways led to nowhere. Railings were installed upside down. Drawers were only one inch deep. Trapdoors were everywhere. Blind chimneys stopped short of the ceiling. There were double-back hallways. Doors opened to steep drops to the lawn below. Many of the bathrooms had glass doors. The list of oddities runs into the dozens. Could there be a more classic example of the ultimate outcome of "building without a purpose?"

We may think that what we are building is not bizarre like Sarah Winchester's construction project. Let me suggest that unless there is a divine purpose behind why we are doing what we are doing, God may actually find it as meaningless and bizarre as the Sarah Winchester Mystery House.

Paul addresses this very issue in 1 Corinthians 3:12-15 when he says,

Now if any man builds on the foundation with gold, silver, precious stones, wood, hay, straw, each man's work will become evident; for the day will show it

because it is to be revealed with fire, and the fire itself will test the quality of each man's work. If any man's work which he has built on it remains, he will receive a reward. If any man's work is burned up, he will suffer loss; but he himself will be saved, yet so as through fire.

May I ask, "What foundation are you building on? What materials are you building with? And *why* are you building what you are building?"

I think John Wesley had it right when he said, "Gain all you can. Save all you can. Give all you can." If we adhere to this compelling "financial triad" as we labor on our building projects, we will be building on a solid foundation utilizing building materials of heavenly "gold, silver, and precious stones." And in our building efforts we will discover that we are indeed living life on purpose.

Some *Food for Thought* Questions

1. In what ways have you been building all these years that might resemble what Sarah Winchester did?
2. What is the purpose behind all your work? What is it supposed to be achieving?
3. How will you know when it is time to stop building your financial empire?

Day 19

Discovering Your Fire Within

The overwhelming majority of people on this planet never really discover the unique life purpose for which God created them. It seems that the materialism and the pursuit of all things good in this life have overshadowed the deeper meaning of our life's purpose. Few people, even serious Christians, are tuned in to the idea of finding and fulfilling their life purpose and divine destiny.

I think this is the reason Rick Warren's *The Purpose-Driven Life* was such a runaway best seller even in secular circles. His book touched a nerve in all of us who want to believe that life in general—and our individual lives specifically—must have some greater meaning and purpose. Oliver Wendell Holmes described the sad futility most people experience when he wrote, "Many people die with their music still in them." In other words, what all these people could have been, and should have been, was never realized.

In the story of Esther, during a secret meeting, her Uncle Mordecai reveals to her a plot to kill all the Jews (of which she is one). What he said to her was hugely profound. He connected this crisis of extinction for the Jews to her unlikely rise to become Queen of Persia. Mordecai asks her, *"And who knows whether you have not attained royalty for such a time as this?"* (Esther 4:14). He was basically saying, "Could it be, Esther, that the reason God made you Queen is because He wants you to save His people from destruction?" Talk about feeling a sense of destiny.

There is something deep within our very beings that nag at us to find some meaning and purpose for our lives. Too often, we try to satisfy this nagging need for purpose by making lots of money, accumulating lots of nice things, being a workaholic, pursuing power and prestige, etc. A multimillionaire told me some years ago—after spending a lifetime dedicated to climbing the ladder of success—that once he had finally reached the top he discovered, to his bitter disappointment, that "the ladder was leaning against the wrong wall." All that he had gained in the climb to "success" was totally overshadowed by what he had lost in its pursuit—his health, his wife, his family, and his friendships.

So, how can we discover what God has really created us to do? There are three areas that must be considered if we are going to find our life purpose.

#1. God has hard-wired into each of us certain God-given passions. These God-given passions are the things that excite us, motivate us, and bring us enjoyment. It may be sports, building things, some moral or social cause, learning, or the arts. Each of us possesses a unique combination of God-given passions. God gave us those passions to point us towards a specific purpose and enable us to fulfill it.

#2. God has given us a unique set of talents. These God-given talents are the things that come naturally to us. For some, it is the ability to sing or teach or an athletic ability or some mechanical insight or understanding. Some people are incredibly artistic, while others have a natural ability to dream of what could be. The way to know you have a God-given talent is that you are better at it than you should be for the time and effort you have put into it. The youth who picks up a basketball and right from the first time he touches the ball he is above average at the game. Or the young lady who captivates all by her singing and yet has never once taken a voice lesson. I had a friend in college who had never taken one piano lesson yet he could sit down and play the piano like he had been taking lessons all his life. He could not read a note of music, but if he could hear the music, he could play it. God has given each of us a unique set of God-given talents for a purpose.

#3. God has planted within each of our hearts some God-given purpose. This God-given purpose has some divine, eternal intention for which we have been created. I am not talking about a general purpose like worshiping Him or living a godly life. These things apply to all of us. I am talking about some specific purpose that He wants us to accomplish for Him with our lives.

When you find something to do with your life that is fueled by your God-given passions, utilizes your God-given talents, and accomplishes a God-given purpose, you will find what I call "the fire within." Engaging in this activity will bring complete fulfillment and will leave you totally energized. It is like when you hit the sweet spot on a baseball bat—you hit a homerun! Now do not think that in order to find your fire within, you need to go into some fulltime Christian work, become a pastor, missionary, or Bible college professor.

Obviously, those are worthy life purposes for those whom God has given the passion, talent, and calling to do those specific kinds of ministries.

Instead, you may be like one Christian man I know. Since he was sixteen years old, he felt called by God to be a businessman. He used his passions and talents coupled with this God-given call to build a very substantial family business. He and his family are now impacting people worldwide with their Christian witness. They also have millions of dollars to give away from the success God has given them. I know another commercial real estate developer who is using his passion for real estate and his talent for making multi-million dollar deals so he can support Kingdom causes that God has laid on his heart. This is his God-given purpose.

Most of you have seen how Tony Dungy, retired coach for the Indianapolis Colts, has used his God-given passion and talent for football as a platform to share the message of Christ with literally millions of people all over the world who would otherwise never step foot into a church building—another worthy God-given purpose.

If you do not want to die with "your music still in you," then I encourage you to discover what God created you for by identifying your God-given passions, your God-given talents, and your God-given purpose. Find something you love and are gifted to do that will fulfill a calling and have an eternal impact. In so doing, you will indeed discover your *fire within*.

Some *Food for Thought* Questions

1. What are the things in your life that you are most passionate about?
2. If you were to ask other people what your greatest gifts are, what do you think they would tell you? Ask them.
3. How can you use your God-given passions and talents to achieve some specific, divine purpose?

Day 20

The Deeper Meaning of Life

If I were to quote the saying, "*It is more blessed to give than to receive,*" would you know who originally said it or where it can be found? It might come as a surprise to you to learn that this statement was made by Jesus. However, it is found in a very unusual place. Whenever you think of the statements of Jesus you immediately think of the Gospels and possibly His few comments in the book of Revelation. But this statement is actually found in the book of Acts 20:35. Paul quotes it in his farewell address to the elders at the church of Ephesus after his three-year ministry with them.

What is particularly interesting about this is that Paul tells the elders to "*remember the words of the Lord Jesus . . . Himself*" suggesting that these words must have been widely known among believers even though they are not recorded in any of the Gospels. The Apostle John does tell us in the last verse of his Gospel, "*Jesus did many other things as well. If every one of them were written down, I suppose that even the whole world would not have room for the books that would be written*" (John 21:25 NIV). So, needless to say, there is much more that Jesus said and did than is recorded in the Bible.

With that as a background, let us consider the verse itself. This verse is just another example of the idea of human contradictions. Jesus was a master of these. He would tell people if they wanted to be first, they would have to be last. If they wanted to live, they would have to die. If they wanted to be rich, they would have to become poor. This is just another in a long list. And this contradiction is nowhere more obvious than at Christmastime when giving and receiving reaches its annual apex.

Just ask a small child whether it is more fun—"blessed"—to get presents at Christmas or to give presents at Christmas, and the answer will always be the same. In fact, they may even look at you with some degree of disbelief. How could you even be asking such a ridiculous question? What keeps young children up at night with excitement is what they are going to *get* the next morning, not what they are going to be *giving*. There is nothing wrong with a child who is almost delirious with excitement about what he will receive—it is very natural. And that is exactly my point. It is very natural. And Jesus is the master of calling us to the unnatural—like loving your enemies and forgiving those who hurt you.

Almost everything about being a follower of Jesus is unnatural or counterintuitive. In fact, it is a safe rule to follow that however you are naturally inclined to respond to a situation, respond just the opposite, and you will probably be responding the right way. You see, the spiritual dichotomy is between what is natural and what is *super*natural—which is how we have been re-born to live. The natural man will say, "It is more blessed to receive than to give." The *super*natural man will say, "It is more blessed to give than to receive."

If we were completely honest with ourselves, we would all admit that it is a blessing to both receive and give. Notice, Jesus said, "It is *more* blessed to give than to receive." When the blessing of receiving overrides the blessing of giving, life becomes warped, myopic, and egocentric.

The story of Ebenezer Scrooge is a classic example of the natural man turned into the supernatural man. Ebenezer's life was consumed with getting and accumulating, while giving was an entirely foreign notion to him. In fact, it could be said he found the idea abhorrent to such an extent that when he was once asked to support the poor so they would not starve to death, he said, "Let them die and decrease the surplus population."

He would squeeze every penny out of every business deal he could, continuing to pile up greater and greater wealth. Yet, his receiving of more and more wealth failed to give him what he was looking for which was true happiness or fulfillment in life. In fact, the more he acquired, the more miserable he became. Something was terribly wrong with this lonely, old man. And the deceitfulness of believing that receiving was the greatest joy had failed him completely. He was not happy. He had no friends. He had no joy.

But then that one fateful Christmas Eve, Scrooge is forced to face himself through three spirits who visit him, and he becomes broken and changed. I mean totally changed—in just one night. How that change manifested itself was in an immediate transformation of his understanding of the purpose for all his accumulated wealth. He now saw it as a resource to be used for doing good. For the first time in his life he gladly opened his hands to help others as quickly and generously as he could. In all his giving he discovered the one truth that had completely eluded him all the years of his life—that it *is* more blessed to give than to receive.

Now this stingy, odious, crabby, hardhearted old man is changed into a generous, pleasant, kind and caring gentleman who finally found tremendous satisfaction in life—no longer in receiving and accumulating wealth for himself, but in giving that wealth in ways that would change people's lives and circumstances.

Sadly, King Solomon's life outcome was not as positive as Scrooge's. As one of the richest men who has ever lived on this planet, Solomon reflects back on all his material accomplishments in Ecclesiastes 12:1-11. Read it carefully.

I said to myself, "Come now, I will test you with plea-sure. So enjoy yourself." And behold, it too was futility. I said of laughter, "It is madness," and of pleasure, "What does it accomplish?" I explored with my mind how to stimulate my body with wine while my mind was guiding me wisely, and how to take hold of folly, until I could see what good there is for the sons of men to do under heaven the few years of their lives. I enlarged my works: I built houses for myself, I planted vineyards for myself; I made gardens and parks for myself and I planted in them all kinds of fruit trees; I made ponds of water for myself from which to irrigate a forest of growing trees. I bought male and female slaves and I had home born slaves. Also I possessed flocks and herds larger than all who preceded me in Jerusalem. Also, I collected for myself silver and gold and the treasure of kings and provinces. I provided for myself male and female singers and the plea-sures of men—many concubines. Then I became great and increased more than all who preceded me in Jerusalem. My wisdom also stood by me. All that my eyes desired I did not refuse them. I did not withhold my heart from any pleasure, for my heart was pleased because of all my labor and this was my reward for all my labor. Thus I considered all my activities which my hands had done and the labor which I had exerted, and behold all was vanity and striving after wind and there was no profit under the sun.

I have always wondered if instead of doing all this stuff "*for myself,*" if Solomon had done these things *for others*, would he have come to the same pessimistic conclusion about his life and his work? "*All [is] vanity and striving after the wind and there [is] no profit under the sun.*" I somehow think not.

With all of Solomon's wisdom, there is one truth that he sadly missed entirely, *"It is more blessed to give than to receive"* (Acts 20:35).

Giving is a natural outgrowth of mature love. We see this so plainly in John 3:16, *"For God so loved..., He gave..."* And we can all be thankful that His desire to receive our gifts of worship and praise was exceeded by His desire to give us a gift that we could never buy for ourselves. Romans 6:23 reminds us that *"the free gift of God is eternal life in Christ Jesus our Lord."*

A biblical approach to life cannot focus simply on maximizing what you will keep for yourself and your family. You must also strive to address the deeper issues of your life's purpose—what can you do to maximize your blessing to others?

It is the introduction of this aspect of giving that brings purpose, meaning, and fulfillment into what would otherwise be nothing more than a set of difficult business decisions that need to be made in order to minimize the damage of taxes. It is this component that gives planning a heart. It is what gives it life.

If you want to experience the deepest meaning in life, let me encourage you to follow the converted Scrooge's example—and not Solomon's—in regards to your accumulated wealth.

Some *Food for Thought* Questions

1. Do you receive more joy when you get things or when you give things? What does this say about your level of spiritual maturity in understanding the deepest meaning of life?

2. How important of a role does giving to others play in your life?

133

3. If you asked ten people who know you well whether they saw you as being more of a giver or a taker, what would they say? Ask ten and find out.

Day 21

Where are All the Wealthy Christians?

Quite recently, I was confronted with a rather startling revelation. It was such a surprise to me that even after considerable reflection, I am still not sure how to process it. The dismaying aspect is that this problem is not new, but rather has been with us from the beginning of Christendom. I had never recognized it before, much less tried to sort out its ramifications. Once I became aware of it, I mentally went back through the plethora of wealthy Christians I have met and worked with over the years, and I was genuinely shocked to see a consistent pattern among the wealthy families I know personally.

Here was my revelation: *the overwhelming majority of wealthy Christians are only marginally involved in their local churches beyond simply attending services.*

I have been blessed to know many wealthy Christians who have a very close personal relationship with God. So it would be inaccurate to conclude that wealthy believers are only marginally committed Christians and their lack of involvement is due to an anemic spiritual life. In fact, I would assert that just the opposite is true. They are serious, committed, in love with Jesus, and living like real believers.

So, how can this be? How is it that we find the overwhelming majority of wealthy Christians routinely disenfranchised from the local church? How is it that these "movers and shakers," these "make it happen" people, these "empire builders" who have a heart for God have somehow found themselves to be a marginalized group in the church? Why are these natural born leaders not leading in the church?

It seems to me that the reasons for this disenfranchisement are much easier to identify than finding effective ways to correct them.

Whether you are part of a wealthy family, minister/pastor of a local church, head of para-church ministry, or professional advisors to the wealthy, I hope you will launch an intentional dialog to identify all the possible causes for the disenfranchisement of wealthy Christians from the local church—and then determine what can be done to draw them into it.

Here are the four areas that I have identified as being, at least in part, the causes of this disenfranchisement.

Cause #1: Senior pastors often feel threatened by wealthy parishioners.

There is no doubt that wealth, power, and influence can be very threatening to a pastor. Generally, pastors are concerned with getting too close to anyone in their church and their wealthiest members might seem even more dangerous than most. If they mess up this relationship, they could lose much more than they might gain from it. It is also very hard for many pastors to relate to someone with substantial wealth.

As I have been pondering this matter, I have noticed that pastors generally do not distinguish between the spiritual aspects and the business aspects of their ministry. As an ordained minister myself who spent four years in Bible college and three years in seminary, I can tell you that of all the classes I had to take in Bible college and seminary, I never took a business, finance, or management class.

A pastor's training is very one-sided. He is generally well equipped to handle the biblical and spiritual aspects of the ministry and often rather ill-equipped to handle the business aspects of ministry. So, instead of attempting to surround himself with people who are experts in operating a business and managing people, they seem to exclude them from any boards or committees. The only two conclusions I can draw is that either they do not want to lose control of that part of their ministry, or they are afraid if a real expert sees what they are doing, they will be criticized. It is one thing for a senior pastor to turn over some of these matters to an associate pastor who answers directly back to him—it is an entirely different thing to turn specific things over to an equal who actually may be vastly more qualified to lead in these areas than the pastor.

Cause #2: The current leadership is suspicious.

The leadership (elders, board of trustees, etc.), which is just a subset of the entire congregation, often seems afraid that if an affluent member were to become part of the board, they would try to take over and run things or start pushing for all kinds of changes that would disrupt the status quo of the church. This often causes the current leadership team to distance themselves from the affluent members.

There is also a general attitude among many Christians (leaders do not seem to be an exception) that if you are rich, you must have done something dishonest along the way. And so the rich are viewed with greater caution.

The fact is that the wealthy do know how to make things grow. They know how to think outside the box. They are not afraid to take calculated risks. And they will make things happen, when others will be afraid to try, instead of seeing these qualities as an invaluable resource to the church. Sadly, the leadership often sees them as something to be avoided.

And so both subtly and even openly, the rich are passed over for leadership roles.

The leadership often has a mindset that this is a church and not a business, and we do not want to run the church like a business. In some areas that is definitely true. But in other areas, a church could learn volumes from the business world in operational efficiency and financial management. There is part of the church that needs to be run like a business and who better to help lead in this area than a successful Christian businessman?

Cause #3: The general congregation is intimidated.

Obviously believers possessing great wealth are always going to be a small minority in any church. In some cases they may even be the only affluent members in the entire congregation. So, right from the start, they are singled out by the congregation as being different because they are rich. Wealthy people tend to intimidate people with more average incomes. Even though my entire ministry is devoted to working with wealthy Christian families, I still on occasion find myself a little intimidated when knowing that I will be meeting someone who is mega-wealthy. My definition of mega-wealthy and yours may be different, but the internal reaction is still the same.

So, wealthy Christians find it very difficult to develop close relationships with people without wealth. Not because the affluent believer has a problem with the common believer, but because the common believer has a problem with the affluent believer. This negative bias I call *wealthism*—as we already discussed on Day 16—has a number of manifestations, all of which work against people of average income being able to forge meaningful and intimate relationships with wealthy Christians.

Cause #4: The church's covert, if not its overt, teaching on wealth is usually faulty.

The evangelical church in general has a very unhealthy attitude about wealth. This attitude is conveyed in hundreds of subtle ways suggesting that there is something wrong with a Christian who has wealth. How often is the verse "money is the root of all kinds of evil" misquoted? We know that it really says the "*love of* money" not just "money," but the common believer just assumes that for anyone to have amassed such a fortune, you must have loved money more than you have loved God (which is a categorically false assumption). Then we hear sermons on the rich young ruler and how when he had to choose between wealth and becoming a disciple, he was unwilling to give up his wealth. Since we are taught to love God more than money, it is the common assumption that any person who is wealthy must be like the rich, young ruler who would not part with his wealth to follow Jesus. We have developed the attitude that poverty and piety go together and that wealth and materialism go together. So, poor is good and rich is bad. The rich get the message from the congregation and occasionally even from the pulpit that "You should feel guilty because you are wealthy."

Of course, the other extreme of this "wealth is bad" attitude is the TV and radio evangelists who proclaim that God wants every believer to be fabulously prosperous—and that it is the right of every believer to be wealthy and all they need to do is "name it and claim it." It is not my intention here to debunk this theology, but I do want to say that it is biblically flawed at its core and leads to its own set of practical difficulties.

So What Can We Do?

What troubles me most about the disenfranchising of wealthy Christians from the local church is that so many of these affluent families are deeply committed Christians who have found ways outside of the church to have a positive impact on our culture and the Kingdom of God. I am blessed and inspired by their faith and their commitment to be godly men and women in the midst of a patently sinful and corrupt world.

I have seen the impact their lives have had over the years and I grieve that so little of what they have to offer the Kingdom gets utilized by their own, local congregations. It is a massive loss for these churches and I would suggest it is time for the church to address this failure. We must find a way to effectively engage some of our most gifted members by allowing them to create and oversee programs for our churches.

I am certain I do not have all the answers on this subject— I am not sure I even know all the questions! While the causes I have mentioned here certainly may not be the only ones that contribute to the marginalization of the wealthy in the church, hopefully this discussion will stimulate your thinking to consider where you are in the life and leadership of your church and why. Once we have better answers to these questions, perhaps we can start to make significant changes to remedy these unnecessary divisions.

Some *Food for Thought* Questions

1. What are your reasons for why you are not more involved in your local church?
2. Do you feel like your church is only interested in your financial support, but really is not looking to engage you in any leadership role? If yes, why?

3. What do you need to do in order to become an important player in the life and ministry of your church using the talents and skills that God has given you?

Day 22

If You Only Had Thirty Days
Left to Live

If you were told that you only had thirty days left to live, you would find this to be a very sobering, if not disturbing, statement, to be sure. You will likely not hear these words in your lifetime, but for the sake of participating in a valuable mental exercise, imagine the following scene:

You are sitting dressed in one of those backless gowns in the examination room at the local hospital after spending all day taking a battery of tests. You are waiting for the doctor to come and give you the results of the tests. He finally walks in. You can tell he is having difficulty looking you in the eyes. The news must not be good.

He sits down next to you and finally looks at you and speaks, "The test results could not be worse. You have a very rare, incurable disease. It is already so advanced that what little treatment we do have would be useless, and there is no surgical procedure known for this illness."

He speaks your name and then slowly says six dreaded words, "You . . . have . . . thirty . . . days . . . to . . . live."

The doctor then adds some extremely good news to his shocking pronouncement, "With the nature of this disease, you will have no negative physical manifestations until the very last day. It will happen all at once, and then it will be over. For the next thirty days, you will continue to feel and look like you do right now. You will notice no change in your

142

current energy level until the very last day. No one will even be able to tell that you are sick."

You weigh his words carefully. You ponder, "I have thirty days to live on this earth before I go on to be with the Lord. Only thirty days!"

Your mind is swirling with the news that your days are numbered. Of course, your days have always been numbered, as is the case for all of us, but your actual number of days remaining has just been revealed to you, and it is several thousand less than you had been assuming.

Once the shock finally sinks in, there is one penetrating question that comes to your mind. The question is this, "What will I do with my last thirty days on the earth?"

"Will I take this month to finally read those books I've wanted to read? Will I go spend these last precious few days with my children and grandchildren? Will I rush back to the office to finish that project that is already past due and absolutely must be finished within the next thirty days? Will I try to 'mend some fences' and 'rebuild some bridges' with people whose relationship with me has been broken or destroyed? Will I finally take that once in a lifetime vacation I've always wanted? Will I go see those people who have influenced and helped me most and tell them 'thank you'? Or will I devote the rest of my days to giving back something of all I have received? And how will I prepare to meet my Father in Heaven?

If you were to face a situation like this, the really important things in life would become obviously apparent. Under such circumstances, it would be easy to distinguish between what is urgent and what is important, what is real and what is superficial and what is lasting and what is temporary.

The great tragedy for far too many of us is that life never becomes more precious than when it is just about over. Then, we hurry around and try to do what has been left undone, fix what has been broken, savor what has been overlooked, and give what has long been overdue.

Few of us will ever be blessed with knowing the exact number of days we have left, so we can "get our house in order" before we say good-bye to this life and those we leave behind. Can you imagine how our priorities might change if we really lived our next thirty days as if they were truly our last? Can you imagine how much more at peace we would be if we actually did those final things *now* instead of waiting until our last thirty days of life arrive?

A gentleman once spoke at a national conference and shared a lesson he had learned from his grandfather. His grandfather told him, "Remember, son, there will be a first time and a last time for everything."

He explained what his grandfather meant. When you kiss your spouse goodbye, there was a first time, and there will be a last time. When you take a walk through the woods, there was a first time, and there will be a last time. When you sit down to a meal with your entire family, there was a first time, and there will be a last time. When you put on your shoes each morning, there was a first time, and there will be a last time. When you hold your child in your arms, there was a first time, and there will be a last time. There will be a first time and a last time for everything.

Being ever mindful of this truth enhances our awareness of life and makes all the "in-between" times far more precious and meaningful. It gives a richness to everyday life that makes it so much sweeter. The fact is you will likely be experiencing a last time of something and not even know it until it has already passed.

The speaker shared that this is what happened to him when he was a teenager and slapped his brother on the back and said "Goodbye" one morning before school. He did not know that he would never be able to say "Goodbye" to him again, because that day his brother would die in an automobile accident.

Let me ask you, "If *you* had just thirty days to live, what would you do with them?"

Some *Food for Thought* Questions

1. What would be your final things to do if you knew you only had thirty days left to live?
2. What will you miss the most once you have done it for the last time?
3. Would it not be better to take care of these final things now so you can be sure all has been done whenever you actually do find yourself living your last thirty days? Why not *just do it*?

Spiritual Thoughts on *Planning*

Now listen, you who say, "Today or tomorrow we will go to this or that city, spend a year there, carry on business and make money." Why, you do not even know what will happen tomorrow. What is your life? You are a mist that appears for a little while and then vanishes. Instead, you ought to say, "If it is the Lord's will, we will live and do this or that."

James 4:13-15 NIV

We should make plans—counting on God to direct us.

Proverbs 16:9 TLB

Day 23

Are Your Advisors Asking You the Right Questions?

Over my nearly three decades of working with wealthy Christian families, I would estimate that about ninety percent of the time these families do not have even one born-again follower of Jesus as an advisor. Sadly, on those rare occasions where they do have a Christian advisor, we find that the advice and planning the Christian advisor has provided is still routinely secular. These Christian advisors have not integrated their personal faith and biblical worldview into their professional practices. In other words, the advice and counsel these Christian advisors are giving their Christian clients is really no different than what their unbelieving counterparts are giving to their clients. The end result is that far too few affluent Christian families have advisors who will help them plan using an overtly Christian, biblical worldview as a foundation.

The crux of the problem is if you do not ask the right questions, you will never get the right answers. Only someone with the same worldview will even think to ask you the right questions. On one occasion, when I was reviewing a proposed Master Stewardship Plan with a family's advisors, the first concern their advisors expressed was that the proposed plan had the family giving away more to Kingdom causes than they were giving to their children. From their secular perspective, the idea of parents giving more of their wealth away to anyone other than their children simply did not compute.

Another advisor suggested that many of his clients choose to pay increased estate taxes in order to increase the amount of the inheritance going to their heirs. However, this couple had already expressly stated that they desired to pay no gift/estate taxes and wanted to maximize their Kingdom giving. This exposed another contradiction between the biblical worldview and the secular worldview adhered to by this advisor.

On another occasion, I had advisors call into question a couple's written goals and objectives. Their response was that these goals and objectives were so extremely contrary to what they understood the family wanted to do, they could not endorse the proposed plan until they confirmed with his client that these goals and objectives were indeed theirs. The advisors then talked with them and confirmed the written goals accurately reflected their wishes.

The reason for this was that the couple's current advisors were operating under a different set of goals and objectives. Because someone coming from a biblical worldview will ask a completely different set of questions and will, consequently, receive a completely different set of answers. Questions coming from a biblical worldview acknowledge:

- God owns everything, and it is our sole job as trustees to find out what God wants us to do with all the stuff He has entrusted to us (see Psalm 24:1);
- it is more blessed to give than to receive (see Acts 20:35);
- "life indeed" comes from being generous and not from holding on to our wealth for our own consumption and pleasure (see 1 Timothy 6:17-19);

- a person's ability to make wealth comes from God and is not the result of our own personal genius and hard work (see Deuteronomy 8:17-18);
- poorly thought out and excessive inheritances can destroy the very people we love the most (see Proverbs 20:21, Ecclesiastes 2:18-19, 21);
- the best financial investment a person can make is in the Kingdom and the "profits" from those investments will be stored up and waiting for us when we relocate to our permanent home to enjoy for eternity (see Matthew 6:19-21); and
- accumulating wealth solely for our own ease and comfort leaves us defined by God as a "fool" (see Luke 12:16-21).

The secular worldview, on the contrary, believes that you want to make all you can, keep all you can, give as much as you can to your heirs, and in that process, pay the least amount of taxes possible. The better you do this, the better you have "played the game."

On more than one occasion I have had secular advisors tell me that it is irrelevant whether the money goes to charity or to the government in taxes because neither directly benefits the family. I could not disagree more. The positive impact on a family, when giving millions of dollars away to worthy Christian organizations and causes is infinitely more beneficial to a family (emotionally and spiritually) than paying that same amount to the Federal Government in unnecessary taxes, which nobody feels good about. The secular worldview focuses only on "me and mine." If something has to go to others, then it does not really matter where it goes.

Let me illustrate my point with a story. A family had created a Master Stewardship Plan that had them giving $17 million to Kingdom causes, paying $0 in gift and estate taxes, and passing $12 million to their kids. The family's secular accounting firm took the "liberty" to rework the plan and suggested to their clients that they had improved on the proposed Master Stewardship Plan. Their new numbers showed $7 million going to charity, $9 million going to the government in taxes, and $13 million going to the children. They claimed their plan design was superior because the children would end up receiving $1 million more with their plan.

Beneficiaries	Creative Plan	Traditional Plan
Kingdom	$17 million	$ 7 million
IRS	$ 0	$ 9 million
Children	$12 million	$13 million

If your worldview believes that how much is given to ministry or paid in taxes are equally irrelevant because neither benefits the family, the accounting firm's plan is indeed better. But from a biblical worldview their "traditional" plan was exceedingly inferior, because they reduced the family's Kingdom giving by $10 million so they could give each of their five children an extra $200,000 that they did not even need.

I estimate that over eighty percent of Christians have made no provision for Kingdom giving. For those few who had, the amount of that giving compared to their net worth was merely a token gesture.

I am convinced it is not that these Christians are not interested in giving, it is because their secular advisors are not asking them the right questions. The fact is, an advisor with a contradictory worldview cannot ask the right questions and consequently a believer will never come to discover the right answers.

Psalm 1:1 clearly states that Christians should not seek the counsel of the ungodly, and this is a perfect example of why. How can you get godly advice from someone who is not godly? How can you get biblical counsel from someone who does not know or believe the Bible? How can you be sure your plans are according to God's will when the advisors who are helping you implement those plans do not personally know God?

Jesus spoke more in scripture about money and material things than He did about sin and salvation. The reason seems obvious to me. Jesus knows where we live. Our stuff is a central part of our everyday lives. As believers, we need to know what the Bible says about financial matters like:

- taxes (see Luke 20:25, Romans 13:7),
- inheritances (see Proverbs 17:16, 19:10a),
- debt (see Proverbs 22:7),
- generous giving (see Luke 6:38),
- accumulating possessions (see Proverbs 18:11),
- investment diversification (see Ecclesiastes 11:1-2),
- hoarding wealth (see Ecclesiastes 5:13),
- financial integrity (see Proverbs 11:1, 10:2a),
- the consequences of planning your life around your stuff (see Matthew 16:26) and
- advice on dozens of other related topics.

It is not enough, however, to just know what the Bible says about such topics, you must also know how to integrate what the Bible says about these things into a comprehensive Master Stewardship Plan that is consistent with all these biblical directives and principles.

So, which of your advisors are asking you the right questions—the important spiritual questions that are consistent with your biblical worldview? Which of your advisors will be able to take the answers to these questions and integrate them into your personal, family, and financial plans so that one day you will be able to hear those blessed words from our heavenly Father, "Well done, thou good and faithful steward?"

If you do not have an advisor who is asking you the right questions, who is able to take the right answers and translate them into a biblically consistent Master Stewardship Plan, you will likely never achieve maximum results for yourself, your heirs, or the Kingdom of God. It is both immediately and eternally worth your time and effort to find such a Kingdom advisor. Let the search begin!

Some *Food for Thought* Questions

1. Are your advisors committed followers of Jesus? Have you ever talked with them about their spiritual walk?
2. Is the counsel your advisors give based upon biblical wisdom or worldly wisdom? How would you know the difference?
3. How can you expect to get godly advice from advisors who do not personally know God or anything about His word? What are you going to do about this?

Day 24

Are You an Informed or an Uninformed Taxpayer?

There is no time of the year when affluent Americans feel more tax-pain than in the month of April. Even if we file extensions to prolong the inevitable, it is still the April 15th deadline that ominously looms over us. Most affluent families are "contributing" between twenty-five to forty percent of their annual income to the Federal Government, a non-profit organization that none of us are really all that excited to support.

I like what the entertainer Arthur Godfrey said, "I'm proud to pay taxes in the United States; the only thing is, I could be just as proud for half the money." And to that I think we would all say, "Amen."

The income and capital gains taxes that are annually extracted from us are not even half of the total tax pain we will ultimately experience. If you are reading this, likely your worst tax bill of all may still be coming.

I recently met with an affluent Christian woman whose very wealthy parents had both eternally relocated that year. Even with the supposed planning of all of their professional advisors, the family was now facing millions of dollars in estate taxes and had very little cash in the estate with which to pay this huge tax bill. As one daughter said, "Mom and Dad have left things in a mess." The estate tax bill is always the biggest pain of all, albeit felt only by those who are left behind.

About forty years ago U. S. Appeals Court Justice, Learned Hand, made this now well known statement, "In America there are two tax systems, one for the informed and one for the uninformed. Both systems are legal."

Uninformed taxpayers reluctantly turn over vastly greater portions of their wealth to the federal government than they need to. Judge Hand goes on to say,

> Anyone may arrange his affairs so that his taxes shall be as low as possible; he is not bound to choose that pattern which best pays the treasury. There is not even a patriotic duty to increase one's taxes. Over and over again the courts have said that there is nothing sinister in arranging affairs as to keep taxes as low as possible. Everyone does it, rich and poor alike, and all do right, for nobody owes any public duty to pay more than the law demands.

U.S. Supreme Court Justice, Louis D. Brandeis, uses a simple illustration to point out our options as taxpayers. He wrote,

> I live in Alexandria, Virginia. Near the Supreme Court Chambers is a toll bridge across the Potomac. When in a rush, I pay the dollar toll and get home early. However, I usually drive outside the downtown section of the city and cross the Potomac on a free bridge. This bridge was placed outside the downtown Washington, D.C. area to serve as a useful social service, getting drivers to drive the extra mile in helping to alleviate congestion during the rush hour. If I went over the toll bridge and through the barrier without paying the toll, I would be committing tax

evasion. If however, I drive the extra mile outside the city of Washington to the free bridge, I am using a legitimate, logical, and suitable method of tax avoidance, and I am performing a useful social service by doing so. For my tax evasion, I should be punished. For my tax avoidance, I should be commended. The tragedy of life today is that so few people know that the free bridge even exists.

His last line is the killer: "The tragedy of life today is that so few people know that the free bridge even exists." You see, informed taxpayers know that capital gains and estate taxes are *optional* and there are "free bridges" they can travel that will allow them to legally avoid them. The informed taxpayer also knows that even though income taxes cannot be eliminated entirely, there are a number of legal and creative planning strategies that will allow them to minimize their annual income tax bill.

Christian families should become informed taxpayers — avoiding all capital gains and estate taxes and paying as little as they possibly can in annual income taxes, so they will have more for themselves, more for their heirs, and more for the Kingdom of God, though not necessarily in that order.

Jesus told us to "...*render to Caesar the things that are Caesar's; and to God the things that are God's*" (Matthew 22:21). Paul adds, "*Render to all what is due them: tax to whom tax is due; custom to whom custom...*" (Roman 13:7). In other words, "if taxes are due, pay them." That is the right thing to do. However, only pay "*what is due*," and not any more. If we are going to be as "*shrewd* [clever] *as serpents and innocent* [honest] *as doves*" (Matthew 10:16), we need to become informed taxpayers who will never needlessly relinquish one penny more of God's money to our government in taxes than we absolutely must.

How are you handling the wealth that God has so graciously entrusted to you? I hope you are managing His wealth as an informed taxpayer.

Some *Food for Thought* Questions

1. What have you done to legally avoid all capital gains and estate taxes since they are entirely optional?
2. How do your current professionals advise you in effectively avoiding, not just deferring, these taxes?
3. If you could give all your capital gains and estate taxes to Christian causes instead of to the Federal Government without reducing your lifestyle or your children's inheritance in any way, would you prefer to do so? What do you need to do to take advantage of this kind of strategic planning?

Day 25

Do Not Render Unto Caesar More than You Owe

Is April 15th anyone's favorite day? I have worked with wealthy families for roughly three decades now and have yet to meet anyone who looks forward with great anticipation to April 15th. I often say that April 15th is the only day that I regret how much money I made the previous year. Many affluent Christians will reluctantly write five to six-digit checks to the IRS on this day. Maybe you were one of them?

Even though your check is written to a not-for-profit organization, the "donation" due on April 15th does not feel anything like a charitable contribution. When we have to write possibly our largest single check of the year to the IRS, no one I have ever met feels good about sending that money to Washington, D.C. never to be seen or heard from again. What is particularly disappointing is that with the size of your "contribution" to this nonprofit organization, they will not even send you so much as a thank you note for your donation!

Even more troubling for those of us who are Christians is that much of what will be done with our "contributions" we will be ethically, morally, and spiritually opposed to supporting. One other thing you can be sure of, they will not be calling us to ask what they should do with our contributions.

I think it is safe to say that of all the things we do with our annual income, our payments to the IRS are the least enjoyable "expenditure." Yet, I have found over the past thirty-plus years that one hundred percent of the families I know have for many years been unknowingly donating substantially more to the IRS annually in income taxes than was necessary.

The Pleasant Surprise of Creative Planning

Most people think that estate planning's primary focus is on the avoidance of estate taxes and effective wealth transfer to the next generation. Indeed, those are key components as they are critically important long-term outcomes that need to be addressed. However, a much more immediate benefit is what results from current tax planning. In fact, reducing income taxes and eliminating capital gains taxes on the sale of appreciated assets should be a far more immediate planning priority than eliminating estate taxes.

Substantial annual income tax savings often comes as a surprise to many families. This tax savings is usually a significant planning "bonus" families had not fully expected when they began the planning process.

Good stewardship demands that we do all we can to legally reduce the income taxes we must pay to the IRS. And let me add that the difference between income tax avoidance and income tax evasion is about fifteen years in Leavenworth! We are talking about tax avoidance here. Employing common, often-used, time-tested, creative-planning techniques will substantially reduce income taxes—all as a direct result of having developed a comprehensive and integrated Master Stewardship Plan.

Real Stories of Income Tax Savings

"The proof is in the pudding," as the old saying goes. So, here are some real life examples of what some families have saved in income taxes. (The names have obviously been changed to protect the wealthy!)

Walter and Sue are independently wealthy and devote their full-time efforts to ministering to pastors in very creative ways. As a result of developing a comprehensive, strategic Master Stewardship Plan, they are now saving an additional $300,000 per year in annual income taxes. This $300,000 now remains in their pockets and under their control instead of going into the coffers of the Federal Government. Consequently, their capacity to minister to pastors has increased by over $300,000 a year!

Tom and Betty were owners of a growing business and needed to develop a strategic Master Stewardship Plan enabling them to (1.) pass on their family business to the next generation who were already involved, (2.) maintain their current lifestyle, and (3.) support Kingdom causes that they really cared about in a significant way. The implementation of their strategic Master Stewardship Plan produced over $230,000 in increased income tax savings for them in the first five years and $700,000 over the rest of their lives.

Rick and Mark together with their wives jointly own a very successful family business. They needed a business continuation plan to get the business to the next generation. They were also facing devastating estate taxes that would severely cripple, if not kill, the business. They were committed Christians who had an earnest desire to support Kingdom causes. They developed an inter-generational Master Stewardship Plan that achieved those objectives. The fringe benefit to the plan was that it saved them over $1.4 million in income taxes over the first five years and almost $11 million over the rest of their lives.

Another significant note in all of these stories is that these families are now going to be giving a combined $200 million away to support the cause of Christ during the rest of their lives and also after they relocate.

In addition to the income tax savings and the increased Kingdom giving from implementing their respective plans, each of these couples' net, spendable incomes actually increased, and their children would now be receiving the exact inheritance they wanted them to have.

All of these positive outcomes were achieved because these families took the time and made the effort to develop a well thought-out, integrated Master Stewardship Plan for themselves and their heirs. Do not think that just because you have a competent accountant you are taking full advantage of all the income tax planning options available to you. That could be a very costly and erroneous assumption.

Some *Food for Thought* Questions

1. How effectively are you minimizing your annual income tax bill? Would you be willing to do additional strategic planning if you could reduce it further?
2. Does your current estate plan produce substantial income tax savings for you each year? If not, why not?
3. What are the barriers that prevent you from becoming more intentional and proactive in taking advantage of diverting even more tax savings to Kingdom causes?

Day 26

How Much Is Enough?

How much is enough? Most affluent people have likely asked this question, but very few have ever taken the time to ask it within a planning context. They rarely ask it of themselves, and they ask it even less frequently in regards to their children's inheritances. But this question must be asked at both of these levels if affluent families want to do the most good with the wealth they have accumulated.

How Much Is Enough for Ourselves?

How much income do you need or want to maintain your current lifestyle for the rest of your life? How much do you need or want in reserve to avoid possible financial disaster in the future? It seems like a simple mathematical equation would give us the answer to the question: "How much is enough for ourselves?"

However, older Americans who lived during the Great Depression have been indelibly marked with the horrible memories of economic collapse and financial ruin—something younger Americans have yet to experience.

These older Americans' first "knee-jerk" reaction to this question is, "We can never have enough because we can never know just how long or how deep the next 'Great Depression' is going to be." Thus, the answer to this question is not a simple mathematical calculation. It requires some lengthy, in-depth conversations to help these people distinguish the facts from feelings as they seek to answer this critically important question.

Affluent families need to address their emotional fears within the context of present reality to help them answer this most basic question: "How much do we need in reserves in order to maintain this present lifestyle until we relocate to be with the Lord?"

How Much Is Enough for Our Heirs?

This question is just as complex and filled with just as much emotion as the first. However, now the emotion is not one of fear, but of love. We have simply gone to the opposite extreme of the emotional continuum.

Warren Buffett may have made the most profound comment on this topic of inheritance. He said, "I want to give my children enough of an inheritance that they will feel like they can do anything, but not so much of an inheritance that they will do nothing."

The overwhelming majority of wealthy parents will concur with this sentiment. Yet almost none of them have tried to identify the minimum and maximum levels of wealth that would be best to pass onto their heirs. Couples need to spend a considerable amount of time answering this most critical question in great detail. Once an affluent individual or couple knows how much wealth is needed to support their desired lifestyle and exactly how much wealth is enough for their heirs, then they are, for the first time, in a financial, emotional and spiritual position to look at their remaining excess wealth. Then they can ask, "What should we do with our surplus?" It is at this point that they can begin to engage in some very meaningful dialog on their level of personal and family giving.

This is what we call the *Psychological Pyramid of Priorities*. It looks like this:

Until the first-level question of "How much is enough for ourselves?" is adequately answered, we cannot go to the next level. Until the second-level question of "How much is enough for our heirs?" is adequately answered, we cannot go to the final level of asking, "How can we give our surplus wealth away to help others?

This Psychological Pyramid of Priorities expresses our most basic human instincts of:

      (1.) taking care of ourselves,

      (2.) taking care of our own, and

      (3.) taking care of others.

Once you understand this Psychological Pyramid of Priorities and move through it, addressing each of the psychological priorities in the proper order, the planning process is not only greatly simplified, it becomes extremely more rewarding than conventional planning.

Some *Food for Thought* Questions

1. What is your current annual lifestyle consumption? Have you discussed this level of consumption with the Lord who is the Owner of your assets?

2. How would you know when you begin consuming more than is pleasing to the Lord? Have you drawn a line that will prevent "lifestyle creep" (spending more as you make more)?

3. If you were to hire someone to manage your assets, what would you be willing to pay him? Is that fee for services comparable to what you personally consume of what God lets you manage of His assets?

Day 27

These are the Times that Try Men's Souls

One might agree that these are the times that try men's souls and how timely these words are in our current economic environment. Yet, they were first penned by Thomas Paine in his work, *The American Crisis*, published in December 1776.

Watching the current stock market plummet and then skyrocket only to plummet again further

—watching every major Wall Street brokerage firm go bankrupt, be bought out, or restructured into a holding bank,

—watching insurance companies, historic bastions of financial security, fall into ruin, only to be saved by billions of dollars of borrowed money provided by the government,

—watching people pay a premium to acquire U.S. Treasuries because they somehow believe that giving money to the greatest debtor nation in history is the safest place to put their money,

—and watching millions of homes fall into foreclosure all around us.

One might agree that these are indeed "times that try men's souls." It seems that there is no place to run. There is no place to hide to avoid the fallout of this current global, financial meltdown. I am reminded of what Jeremiah said about Israel in Jeremiah 6:14. They cry out, *"Peace, peace, but there is no peace."*

If you have not fretted even a little bit over the torrent of disastrous economic news that seems to assault and affect us daily, you are to be commended. But dare I say for the rest of us, we have spent a disproportionately large amount of time these past months addressing emotionally and financially the personal ramifications of all that is unraveling around us.

In tumultuous times like these, it may be most appropriate for each of us to take a personal inventory of what we really believe and how consistently we are living out our beliefs. There are three foundational beliefs many of us may have been reminded of recently that have possibly betrayed us.

"I Am Not in Control"

"Control freaks" is a common term used to describe many of us. *Control* is one of our most important concerns and giving up control of anything is very difficult for control freaks. In times like these, we are reminded just how little control we actually have of anything in life. For an unbeliever this can be a shattering reality, but for those of us who are believers, we ought to sigh in relief and acknowledge that even though we are in control of very little, our Father is in control of everything and He loves and cares for us. God is not sitting in Heaven wringing His hands, muttering, "Oh, my! What am I going to do about this mess?" God is sovereign and nothing happens on this planet that is not either caused by Him or permitted by Him. That will be good news if we have bought into desiring His agenda more than our own.

Our anxiety comes when we see our agenda in jeopardy, which mostly is based upon a fear that something may happen that would prevent us from maintaining the lifestyle with which we have grown comfortable. 1 John 4:18 reminds us that, *"perfect love casts out fear."* Faith in God and fear of uncertainty are incompatible. You either have faith or you have fear. You cannot have both.

In times such as these, we are reminded that we are not in control of the events of life. We will be forced to determine if our faith in a sovereign, all-loving, and all-knowing God is really the cornerstone of who we are or just some spiritual platitudes that have not really taken root in how we live our daily lives.

"I Am Trusting Too Much in the Stuff and Not Enough in the Owner"

When you see the value of your retirement plans, your investment portfolio, or your real estate holdings substantially dropping in value, how do you react? Does it cause a degree of churning in your gut? After all, this is all God's stuff and we are not dependent solely on the stuff that has our name on it, but on all the stuff that has God's name on it.

Paul had a very profound comment in Philippians 4:11b-12. He admits,

> *...I have learned to be content in whatever circumstances I am. I know how to get along with humble means, and I also know how to live in prosperity; in any and every circumstance I have learned the secret of being filled and going hungry, both of having abundance and suffering need.*

Paul is telling us that contentment has nothing to do with the amount of stuff we have accumulated. If that were the case, he would have been content with prosperity and discontent with humble means. So, what is this secret that Paul has learned about contentment? I think it is this, "Contentment does not come from what we have or do not have; it comes from *who has us!*" If our trust is in our Owner and not in our stuff, whether the stuff goes up or down in value, or goes away altogether, it has no impact on our contentment in life.

"I Am Focused Too Much on this Life and Not Enough on the Next"

We are not the first to be subtly seduced into focusing too much attention on this life. Paul reminded the Colossians in 3:2 to, "*Set your minds on things above, not on earthly things*" (NIV). It is easy enough to be "earthly" focused, is it not?

We must never forget that we leave this world the same way we came into it—with nothing. Solomon reminds us in Ecclesiastes 5:15, "*As he had come naked from his mother's womb, so will he return as he came. He will take nothing from the fruit of his labor that he can carry in his hand.*"

Tony Campolo tells a story about when he was taking his young son on a bus tour through Chicago. As the bus pulled up to an alley, the tour guide pointed to the alley and said, "This is the alley where Al Capone was shot down and of all the millions of dollars that he had stolen, when he died he had only thirty-five cents left to his name."

Tony's son looked at him and said, "What great timing!"

You go out the same way you came in. As John Ortberg says, "When you die, like when the monopoly game is over, it all goes back in the box for someone else to play with after your game is over."[3]

This life only causes us anxiety when we lose sight of the next. One of my favorite choruses growing up says it all:

[3] Ortberg, John, *When the Game Is Over It All Goes Back in the Box*. Grand Rapids, MI: Zondervan, 2007.

This world is not my home; I'm just 'a passin' through.
My treasures are laid out, somewhere beyond the blue.
The angels beckon me from Heaven's open door,
And I can't feel at home in this world anymore.

As Martin Luther King once said, "There are only two days on my calendar—*today* and *that* day." May each of us do all we can to never lose sight of both of these days as we seek to successfully navigate through the many temporary troubles of this life.

Some *Food for Thought* Questions

1. How affected are you by fear and anxiety of circumstances and events that are outside your control?
2. Would those who know you characterize you as a control freak? How does that align with being a follower of Christ and a steward of His resources?
3. When times are difficult how do you maintain a sense of security? How well does it work for you?

Spiritual Thoughts on *Inheritances*

A good man leaves an inheritance.

Proverbs 13:22

Wisdom along with an inheritance is good and an advantage to those who see the sun. For wisdom is protection just as money is protection.

Ecclesiastes 7:11-12

Day 28

Casting a Shadow Beyond the Grave

Mankind is mortal. God has granted us a certain number of days to dwell upon this earth. For some, it may be only a few days. For others, it may be tens of thousands of days. No matter what our number, there will come a time for all of us when our last day will arrive. Then this life, as we now know it, will be over.

At that point, who we were and what we did in our lives will be permanently fixed in the minds of those who knew us. There will be no more additions to those memories. No corrections. No modifications. Our relationships with people, our actions, what was important to us, how we lived our lives, and how we used our resources will now be unchangeably etched in the memories of all those who knew us. The final paragraph of the final chapter of our book will have been written and the indelible ink will have dried.

How fondly will you be remembered by those who knew you? Will you be someone people will even want to remember? Will you be someone people will be glad to forget? Most of us hope that once our days have played out and we are gone, someone will remember us with gratitude and affection. Something of what we have done in our lives will survive us and serve to one degree or another as a meaningful monument to our brief pilgrimage on this planet.

As I consider all of this, I am reminded once again of the gripping story of Ebenezer Scrooge. He was a tight-fisted, cold-blooded, calculating business man who had amassed an incredible fortune yet still continued to squeeze every penny he could out of everyone with whom he dealt. His goal was to become rich and consequently to become happy, and he had achieved his financial goal several times over. Yet, there was never enough money because he still was not happy. So he continued to amass ever-greater piles of gold. The means—gaining wealth—had subtly shifted to the end in and of itself.

One cold Christmas eve, Ebenezer is given a gift from his old, deceased business partner, Jacob Marley. His gift was a chance to see his life from a different perspective. Following the visitation of three spirits, Ebenezer faces himself as a broken and empty shell of a man.

The most gripping scene in the story is when Ebenezer is kneeling over his own gravestone after seeing everyone's disdain and disrespect of him after his death. Ebenezer appeals to the "Spirit of Christmas Future" to assure him that what he has seen is not unchangeably fixed for eternity, but can be changed and that the outcome of his life might be different than the horrors he has witnessed. After seeing beyond his days, he desperately regretted the way he lived. He pleads with the spirit to give him a chance to go back and to do things differently. With indescribable gratitude, he awakens on Christmas morning in his own bed—alive!

In one short night, this miserable, stingy, odious man is radically transformed into one of the most caring, generous, and gracious men ever known by the people of London. Not only did he use his wealth and his life to bless the lives of countless people from that point forward, he also, for the first time in his life, found the true happiness that had continually eluded him before. He had finally come to understand the words of Jesus, "*It is more blessed to give than to receive*" (Acts 20:35).

Sadly, or maybe gladly, none of us will be given the supernatural opportunity to go beyond our grave and look back to see how our life impacted others. Many of us might be greatly distressed if we did. I am not sure we really need to do that in order to grasp the full scope of the shadow we are casting. If we would be totally honest with ourselves, it should not be too difficult to get some idea of the size and length of the shadow that we are casting and just how enduring it will be.

However, for those who are concentrating on making a difference—"casting a shadow," if you will—we will never fully comprehend the length and breadth of our own shadows. So often, what we give of ourselves to others ends up getting passed around and typically impacts the lives of many people we will never know. The Apostle Paul is an excellent example of this. I am certain that Paul had no idea that tens of millions of people would be eternally impacted by the shadow his life has cast throughout the ages.

If you are going to "cast a shadow" beyond your own days, you must invest your time, your money, and your interest in things and people that are outside of yourself. What are you doing with your life and resources to cast a shadow that will stretch beyond your grave? Keep in mind, you will not be remembered by what you have kept for yourself—you will be remembered by what you have given to others! The only place you cannot cast a shadow is on yourself.

Some *Food for Thought* Questions

1. Who will remember anything about you one hundred years from now?
2. How comfortable are you with the legacy you will be leaving behind for those who survive you?
3. Of all the things that you want to be remembered for, which would be the most important?

Day 29

Inheritances: Oh, What to Do?

Of all the issues that affluent parents confront in planning, none consumes more time and emotional energy
than that of inheritances—and for good reason. There is
no area of the planning that could be more devastating to a
family than an ill-thought out or ill-timed inheritance. Over
the past several decades, I have had the opportunity to review
hundreds of estate plans. In all those years, I have yet to see
a current inheritance plan that parents were entirely happy
with when their outcomes were explained to them.

In one case, the parents said they only wanted their
children to get a lifetime income stream because they were
opposed to giving lump sum inheritances. Their attorney
drafted the documents so the children would receive an
income stream for life. Since no directive was discussed
for what to do with these income-producing trusts after the
children died, the attorney designed the trusts so the grandchildren (some of whom were not even born yet) would get
an outright distribution of the trust assets when the children
died. The grandchildren were going to become lump sum
multimillionaires. The parents were mortified when they
actually saw their current plan mapped out.

With a couple of other families, when the parents saw
exactly what their children were going to inherit, they were
so shocked and concerned they immediately called their
attorney and changed their wills before leaving on extended
vacations.

When another couple saw the excessive amount that their current plan was going to provide for their children, the father jumped up from his chair, ran to the screen where the presentation was being projected, pointed to the box on the flowchart showing the amount going to the children and cried out, "Look at what they are going to get! I cannot believe it. Look at that! We've got to do something about that."

How does this kind of thing happen? I would suggest that all of these families had very good legal and accounting professionals who attempted to serve them well. However, if clear directives from the parents are not provided, legal documents typically end up with standard, boilerplate, inheritance language that is anything but carefully and strategically thought out for the family's unique situation.

Here are just a few of the many complex issues that make inheritance planning such a challenging conundrum for families.

Conundrum #1

All our children are not the same in their readiness to handle a sizeable inheritance. However, we feel obligated to treat them all the same because we love them all the same and do not want to be perceived as showing favoritism.

Conundrum #2

Some of our children are involved in our family business and others are not, yet the vast majority of our wealth is tied up in the company. How do we treat them all fairly when not all of them will get the business?

Conundrum #3

We would like to leave our grandchildren an inheritance, but we do not want to override the influence of their parents by giving an inheritance directly to the grandchildren.

Conundrum #4

We have one child that is not living a lifestyle of which we approve. We do not know how to address these inheritance issues with our "black sheep," and it also significantly affects how we are able to plan for our "good" children.

Conundrum #5

Our children are all extremely different and do not get along that well. If we simply divide all our property up equally among them, family conflict will be inevitable.

As you can see these are exceptionally complex issues and there are no quick fixes or boilerplate solutions to these conundrums. It will take a lot of time, a lot of prayer, and a lot of conversations to create a strategic inheritance plan that will actually bless, and not create unseen problems for your heirs.

As I was visiting with a very wealthy Christian couple a number of years ago, I asked them the question, "How much is enough for your children?" The husband responded quite quickly and said, "I want each of our five children to get $10 million dollars." However, this total inheritance was only a small portion of his total wealth.

I asked him how he arrived at this amount. He reached his hand to the sky and grabbed a handful of air, pulled it down, opened his hand before me and said, "I kind of came up with it out of thin air. It just seemed like a nice round number."

I said, "Well, let's think about that amount for a minute. If they each got $10 million and put it in a relatively conservative investment yielding five percent a year that would give them an annual income of about $500,000 or about $10,000 a week. This amount of income should enable them to sit on their couch and watch TV everyday for the rest of their lives never doing anything productive or meaningful." The wife gasped and said, "Honey, I'm not sure that is the right amount."

I asked him, "Do you want to fund opportunity or lifestyle for your children?" He answered, "Opportunity." Then I said, "There is a huge difference between funding opportunity and funding lifestyle. Exactly what do you want your inheritance to do for your children?" This one question led to two more hours of inheritance discussion.

Most families spend far more time preparing the legal documents for their children's inheritance than they do actually preparing their children for their inheritance. If you want a successful inheritance plan, what you do around the kitchen table with your family is far more important than what you do around the conference table at your attorney's office.

Ecclesiastes 7:11-12a says, *"Wisdom along with an inheritance is good and an advantage to those who see the sun. For wisdom is protection just as money is protection."* What are you doing to give your heirs the *wisdom* they need to handle the wealth you intend to give them?

I have adapted the Maturity Marker work done by Mitchell Baris, Carla Garrity, and Carol and John Warnick into four biblically based Maturity Markers to help parents more objectively assess the preparedness of their heirs to successfully handle their desired inheritances.

Unfortunately, parents typically address their inheritance dilemmas by executing legal documents that attempt to protect their ill-prepared heirs from harming themselves with their coming inheritance. With the use of these four

Maturity Markers, however, parents are able to address and work to correct the problem areas in their heir's lives.

A primary inheritance objective in our working with families is to "stop the bleeding" and heal the "wound," not simply put a "legal bandage" on a currently infected character defect hoping that somehow the "patient" will at least not get any worse in the future.

Spiritual Maturity Marker #1
(An Heir's Relationship with God)

Signs for this Spiritual Maturity Marker would include an heir who is...
- (1.) growing as a personal follower of Jesus;
- (2.) developing in godly character; and
- (3.) ministering to others.

Emotional Maturity Marker #2
(An Heir's Relationship with Himself)

Signs for this Emotional Maturity Marker would include an heir who is...
- (1.) taking responsibility for his/her actions and proactively seeking to correct his/her mistakes and sins;
- (2.) controlling his/her anger, frustration, disappointment, and stress appropriately; and
- (3.) avoiding chronic problematic and self-destructive behavior.

Relational Maturity Marker #3
(An Heir's Relationship with Others)

Signs for this Relational Maturity Marker would include an heir who is...

(1.) developing and maintaining healthy and meaningful long-term relationships with friends and family;

(2.) treating other people with respect and dignity; and

(3.) making personal sacrifices for the benefit of others.

Financial Maturity Marker #4 (An Heir's Relationship with Money)

Signs for this Financial Maturity Marker would include an heir who is...

(1.) living financially independent of parents;

(2.) exercising consumptive self-control in spending; and

(3.) engaging in enthusiastic and generous giving.

These maturity markers should better equip you to have real, meaningful dialog with your children enabling you to establish measurable and attainable standards by which to make more objective inheritance decisions instead of having those decisions driven primarily by emotion and guilt. As you can see, coming up with a thoughtful, loving, and effective inheritance plan for your family is neither simple nor easy; but, without a doubt, it will be time very well spent for you and for your family.

Some *Food for Thought* Questions

1. What inheritance conundrums are you struggling with?

2. How prepared are your children/grandchildren to receive the inheritance you intend to give them?

3. How certain are you that your current planned inheritance will actually end up blessing and not cursing your family?

Day 30

Preparing Your Heirs for Their Inheritance

One of the greatest struggles that wealthy parents seem to have is, "How can we effectively pass our wealth on to our heirs without ruining them?" The fact is that an ill-planned inheritance can actually ruin the very ones you love the most. This parental concern is not new to our day either. It has troubled the wealthy for thousands of years. King Solomon (circa 700 BC), a man whose wealth is legendary, struggled with this very issue. He expressed his concern over this frustrating dilemma when he confessed:

> *Thus I hated all the fruit of my labor for which I had labored under the sun, for I must leave it to the man who will come after me. And who knows whether he will be a wise man or a fool? Yet he will have control over all the fruit of my labor for which I have labored by acting wisely under the sun. This too is vanity.*
> *Ecclesiastes 2:18-19*

Is there a way to affect the outcome of whether our children will be wise or fools with their inheritances? The answer is, "Definitely, yes!" But, as in all other areas of family wealth planning, the best planning is done while you are still alive.

Consider the exposure unplanned wealth can create for an heir. Suddenly your heirs are wealthy. How can they know whether people are genuinely interested in them or merely interested in enjoying the benefits of their wealth? Remember, the wealthy will always have many "friends." Your heir may eventually begin to question, "Do you love me or my money?" This uncertainty can be destructive to a person's self-image.

Also, heirs risk becoming obsessed with self-consumption. Their whole world can begin to revolve around their individual wants, turning them into the well-known and little-regarded "spoiled, rich kid." The younger an heir is when they receive their unearned inheritance, the greater the chance of this outcome.

Further, they risk losing the important connection between work and reward. They have been rewarded for doing nothing except being born into the right family and surviving the older generations. Not exactly a major accomplishment.

So, how can you pass this wealth onto your heirs without making them insecure, lazy, and/or spoiled rotten? *You teach them about generosity!*

Why not immediately establish a family foundation, fund it with a specific sum, and then charge these future heirs with the task of distributing these funds to worthy charitable causes? (If you focus your philanthropic efforts in third world countries, much can be done with relatively little money.)

You might ask, "What will this teach them?" What they will learn from this experience, especially if repeated frequently during your remaining lifetime, is significant. For example, imagine what it would feel like for your heirs to know that they have built an orphanage in Guatemala that will house twenty orphan children and will also feed them for the next five years for only $15,000.

Knowing that they have made a difference in the lives of twenty needy children will be profoundly fulfilling for your heirs. Even though they did not use any of their own money, they still, amazingly, gain almost all the emotional and psychological benefits of this philanthropic project, just as if they had put up the money themselves. They say, "Look what we did!" not, "Look what mom and dad (or grandma and grandpa) did!"

You have helped improve their self-image, directed their focus away from selfishness, and enabled them to do a meaningful work. What a powerful combination of benefits for such a small investment.

The goal then is to repeat this kind of philanthropic activity often enough that it becomes a way of life for your heirs. Then once they finally receive their inheritance the typical problems created by inherited wealth can be avoided.

The Power of Giving

In separate meetings with two very wealthy couples, I asked them this question, "What is the most meaningful charitable gift you have ever made?" The first shared that it is the $240 that they annually give to sponsor a child in Africa. The other couple said it was the $500 they send each year to the Salvation Army orphanage in Mexico near where they frequently vacation. Both of them have over $1 million in annual income and a net worth of over $10 million, yet both couples admitted that these insignificant, annual gifts were providing them with considerable personal satisfaction.

How can an annual gift of so little be so meaningful? It is the simple fact, "What comes back to you from charitable giving is always disproportionate to the size of the gift you make." It is always disproportionate regardless of whether you are giving away $240 or $2.4 million. If this is true for wealthy parents, it is also true of the children and grandchildren of wealthy parents.

Generosity builds character, develops a positive self-image, and provides a real sense of accomplishment in those who participate in it. So, consider beginning a significant giving program now and include all the heirs in your family. It will not only be a growing experience for both you and your heirs, it can also become a wonderful activity that will draw your family together in a way that no other family activity can. You have nothing to lose with this stewardship giving strategy except your concern over how successfully your heirs will handle their inheritance when it comes.

Some *Food for Thought* Questions

1. How aware are your children of your giving?
2. On a 1-10 scale, how generous are your children? Are you happy with that rating?
3. How do you feel about the idea of doing your Kingdom giving as a family?

Other Books by E. G. "Jay" Link

To Whom Much is Given: Navigating the Ten Life Dilemmas Affluent Christians Face. Longwood, FL. Xulon Press, 2009. (Available at www.KardiaPlanning.com or Amazon.com.)

Family Wealth Counseling: Getting to the Heart of the Matter. Franklin, IN. Professional Mentoring Program, 1999. (Available at www.KardiaPlanning.com or Amazon.com.)

Kardia, Inc.
5237 SR 144
Mooresville, IN 46158
317-831-7200
www.KardiaPlanning.com

Worthwhile Additional Reading

Alcorn, Randy C. *The Law of Rewards*. Wheaton, Ill: Tyndale House, 2003.

Alcorn, Randy. *The Treasure Principle: Unlocking the Secret of Joyful Giving*. Sisters: Multnomah, 2005.

Beckett, John D. *Loving Monday: Succeeding in Business Without Selling Your Soul*. New York: InterVarsity Press, 2006.

Blue, Ron, and Jeremy White. *Splitting Heirs: Giving Your Money and Things to Your Children Without Ruining Their Lives*. Grand Rapids: Northfield, 2008.

Buford, Bob. *Finishing Well: What People Who Really Live Do Differently!* New York: Integrity, 2005.

Buford, Bob. *Game Plan*. Grand Rapids: Zondervan, 1999.

Buford, Bob. *Halftime: Changing Your Game Plan From Success to Significance*. Grand Rapids: Zondervan, 1994.

Grudem, Wayne. *Business for the Glory of God: The Bible's Teaching on the Moral Goodness of Business.* New York: Crossway Books, 2003.

Stanley, Andy. *Fields of Gold.* New York: Tyndale House, 2004.

Tam, Stanley. *God Owns My Business.* New York: Horizon Books, 1991.

Organizations That Can Continue to Challenge Your Spiritual Thinking

Crown Financial Ministries
(www.Crown.org)

Eternal Perspective Ministries
(www.EPM.org)

Excellence in Giving
(www.ExcellenceinGiving.com)

The Gathering
(www.TheGathering.com)

Generous Giving
(www.GenerousGiving.org)

Halftime
(www.Halftime.org)

Kingdom Advisors
(www.KingdomAdvisors.org)

National Christian Foundation
(www.NationalChristian.com)

Pinnacle Forum
(www.PinnacleForum.com)

Waterstone
(www.LivingDefined.org)

CPSIA information can be obtained
at www.ICGtesting.com
Printed in the USA
LVOW12*2123221216

518469LV00003B/6/P